WORCESTERSHIRE'S
MOTORING HERITAGE

WORCESTERSHIRE'S MOTORING HERITAGE

MARTIN WATTS

AMBERLEY

First published 2014

Amberley Publishing
The Hill, Stroud
Gloucestershire, GL5 4EP

www.amberley-books.com

British Library Cataloguing in Publication Data.
A catalogue record for this book is available from the British Library.

ISBN 978 1 4456 0419 0 (print)
ISBN 978 1 4456 3714 3 (ebook)

Typeset in 10pt on 12pt Sabon.
Typesetting and Origination by Amberley Publishing.
Printed in the UK.

Contents

Introduction

When recounting the historical significance of Worcestershire, historians often focus their attentions upon the part played by the county in the English Civil War; its pedigree as one of the world's finest producers of porcelain, bearing that famous 'Royal Worcester' stamp; the intriguing and secretive sauce produced by Lea & Perrins; its majestic cathedral, which nestles on the banks of the river Severn; the birthplace of England's greatest composer, Sir Edward Elgar; and Malvern mineral water, once the favourite tipple of her majesty Queen Elizabeth II. In highlighting these important names and their links to this great county, one is only just scratching the surface of historical gems, and yet the county played a major part in motoring history through the twentieth century and it is often only the name of the Morgan Motor Company which is recalled on so many occasions in relation to the county's motoring heritage.

As a child growing up in and around the City of Worcester during the 1950s and 1960s, I was fortunate enough to have relatives who would feed my mind with historical facts and figures, anecdotes and tales. My grandfather, an ex-Worcester City Policeman, would recount his eerie feelings at having to patrol through the cathedral during the night on his own during the wartime period; his memories of the early trams through the city had me listening intently. I also recall visiting my great-grandfather's gun factory, which stood only a short stroll away from the cathedral, on the edge of the Severn, a spot now occupied by the college car park. My great-great-grandfather once owned and worked the flour mill at Mildenham Mill on the outskirts of Worcester, another fascinating place that I visited as a child; I only found out many years later that my great-great-grandfather had a carriage produced by McNaughts in the Tything, a company who had hand-crafted the Lord Mayor's coach used in London. The tales and memories generated by my childhood experiences are, I suspect, largely responsible for my keen interest in history, though it would be motoring history which fired my imagination as I grew older.

It was my enthusiasm for Grand Prix racing which was responsible for my escalating interest in the general motoring history of Worcestershire as I grew older. Realising that the county had far more links to motor racing than I had at first envisaged, I began to dig deeper into the county's links with the motor car and its evolution throughout the twentieth century. Little did I realise, when listening to my late grandfather's tales of the Worcester tram siege or seeing the Williams Grand Prix car with the 'Wards' (of Worcester) sponsorship logo in the early 1970s, that such fleeting moments in my life would take me on a motoring voyage of discovery around the county many years later. I grew up in the county thinking, like so many, that it was famous only for the things already mentioned in my opening diatribe; how wrong can one be? The county has always had strong links to the motoring industry, with many companies being major suppliers of vehicle components, tooling and testing equipment. Adjust your seat and fasten your seatbelt, and come and join me on a sojourn through the many Worcestershire motoring connections.

1

The Motoring Pioneers of Malvern – Santler

When beginning such an epic motoring journey through the county, there is without doubt no better place to start than in my adopted home town of Malvern, a place which I visited often in my early years from my Worcester home. Malvern is a quaint spa town nestling on the slopes of the glorious Malvern Hills, popularized by its mineral water qualities; many were attracted to its wells both to drink and douche their bodies in order to heal ailments and infirmities. The wells, water cure establishments and hotels of the area were visited by many famous people, who included Charles Dickens, Charles Darwin, Princess Victoria, Errol Flynn and countless other notables. As a town more noted for its picturesque landscape and far removed from the industrial towns to the north of the county, it often intrigues me as to why Malvern came to play such a vital role in Britain's motoring history. If the town of Malvern is mentioned within motoring circles, then it is the name of the Morgan Motor Company which is at the forefront of a person's mind, and yet Malvern's connection with the automotive industry goes far beyond the wonderful sports cars produced by Morgan.

It was during the 1990s that the name of Santler first came to my notice: a small company based in Malvern who had an engineering concern producing a variety of machinery, from bicycles to motorised farming ploughs. I became intrigued by the Santler brothers, Charles and Walter, and discovered through some research that they had produced what they claimed was to be the first British car, initially steam driven and later adapted to a petrol-driven example. The story became ever more intriguing when, to my delight, I learned that

Charles claimed to have visited Karl Benz in Germany and worked with him on the world's first motor car (a claim never verified, sadly). From this moment I was completely hooked by the Santler story, and yet slightly baffled as to why there was no permanent reminder of the company's achievements in my home town. We have a great tradition in the UK of being able to honour famous people and events in our history in a variety of ways, such as a blue plaque, a road name or a dedicated section within a local museum, but nothing was to be found in Malvern to honour the Santler name. Those pre-internet days of research were by no means easy, and as any historian will tell you, they involved a lot of leg work, library visits and endless hours of searching through local records, old newspapers, regional directories/gazetteers and trade publications. Slowly but surely I began to build up a picture of the Santler brothers and their engineering business in Malvern. It was around this time that a feature appeared in a national newspaper, a story about Britain's earliest surviving motor car, referred to as the 'Malvernia'. This was music to my ears, as not only had the pioneering brothers produced the first UK car, but it had survived, having been discovered in a disused blacksmith's shop only a short distance from where it was built nearly 100 years prior; a remarkable story.

I managed to find an address for the owner of the vehicle and made contact with him, explaining that for the previous couple of years I had been researching the Santler company and their products. I was overwhelmed by the very long letter I received from the owner, explaining in detail everything about the motor car, how it was discovered and restored, and better still some fascinating details of the Santler brothers which I was unaware of.

Previous generations were accustomed to following the trade skills of their parents, usually the father, and this appears to have been the case with the Santler brothers, Charles and Walter. Their father, Thomas Santler, ran an engineering business from Quest Hills, Malvern Link, and by 1885 the business had incorporated electrical engineering into its portfolio, along with the manufacture of cycles from the Northumberland Works in Quest Hills. It is the elder Santler brother, Thomas 'Charles', who has been credited in recent years with being the innovative designer of the brothers. Charles was educated at the Lyttleton Grammar School in Malvern, later becoming an apprentice engineer to William Dean, based at the Swindon site of the Great Western Railway. Records indicate that Charles later underwent a further period of study at Birmingham College of Science before returning to his hometown of

Malvern to continue in the family engineering business. The inventive design skills of Charles had already been put to good use during his time of study at Birmingham because in 1879 he invented a free-wheeling modification to the treadle of a small lathe which was in use at the college. He would later take out a patent for this design, which he adapted for use on a bicycle in partnership with a John Nicholls of Malvern. When fitted to a bicycle with 30-inch wheels, several experimental runs were made from the Malvern factory to the village of Ombersley (over 20 miles). Further tests were conducted on the bicycle between the factory and Presteigne, a round trip in the region of 60 miles.

By the mid-1880s the Santler family had expanded their engineering and electrical business into the manufacture of bicycles at the Northumberland Works in Howsell Road. By 1890 the Santler catalogue contained several examples, such as 'The Malvern Cripper' tricycle for £20, 'The Malvern Safety No. 1' at £14 and 'The Malvern Safety No. 2' for £16. Charles and Walter were themselves very keen cyclists, being early members of the Malvern Cycling Club, formed in 1883. Still running alongside the bicycle production at this time was their engineering concern, which included the installation of steam and gas engines, plus the fitting of electricity generating turbines in both commercial and residential premises. By 1896 the Santler engineering and cycle business had outgrown the premises in Howsell Road, so production was moved to larger facilities on the Worcester Road in Malvern Link: the 'Malvernia Works'.

With the brothers' combined engineering skills, a natural progression would lead them to build a two-cylinder, vertical steam powered, four-wheeled carriage in 1889, which they tested on private roads at the Madresfield Estate, close to Malvern Link. The steam engine in this carriage was replaced by an internal combustion engine, and by 1894 the brothers were claiming to have achieved speeds of around 12 mph. It has further been claimed in period motoring publications that such was his interest in self-propelled road vehicles that Charles had collaborated with Karl Benz on the world's first car, but no evidence exists to support this claim made by Charles.

Charles Santler stated in an interview in later life that the 1889 carriage was laid up at Newland (on the approach to Malvern Link) in 1900, in a blacksmith's yard to the rear of The Swan public house. By 1897 the Santler brothers had added motorcycles to their catalogue.

As part of Malvern's celebrations to mark the coronation of George V in 1911, the Santler carriage (minus the engine) was dragged from its resting place behind the blacksmith's yard in order for it to form part of a procession in the town. A notice on the front of the carriage read, 'Ye Old Malvern Trackless Car'. It appears that after this event, the carriage most likely went back into storage until it was discovered by John Mills of Leamington during the 1930s. Mr. Mills did manage to meet and talk with the car's designer, Charles Santler, who was able to give him background information and even some paperwork relating to the vehicle. During the 1950s Mr Mills sold the unrestored Malvernia to a Mr Alec Hodgson, a musical instrument maker and veteran car restorer. Mr Hodgson installed a Benz engine in the vehicle, and in addition made some alterations to the frame, running gear and bodywork. The Malvernia would pass into the ownership of several more people, including Sir John Briscoe, before being acquired by a doctor in 1985. The doctor undertook many hours of painstaking research into the Santler company, and it is thanks to his endeavours that we know so much about the Santler products and the company history today. He produced a book as a result of his extensive research, entitled *Malvernia*, and this was published in 1987 by the Michael Sedgwick Memorial Trust. The Veteran Car Club (UK) dating committee later concluded as a result of this thorough research that the Malvernia was probably constructed in 1894, and they further concluded that a more appropriate title/name for the vehicle was the 'Santler'.

The Santler brothers have cemented their place within Britain's motoring history due to the design and construction of the 'Santler' vehicle, and yet the factory continued to produce mechanical goods into the twentieth century. An improved vehicle was constructed at the factory in the form of a 6-hp front-engined model with a Phaeton body, and this was registered in 1904. It is believed that this example was later fitted with a four-seater tonneau body. During this period, the brothers and their factory workforce continued to offer their skills as general engineers and electrical specialists, plus the continued bicycle production. By this time they had also added motor car repairs and the sale of petrol to their list of services and were attracting the patronage of several wealthy enthusiasts from the Malvern area, including W. Dyson Perrins, who owned quite a stable of expensive motor cars.

Shortly before the outbreak of the First World War, the Santler brothers introduced the 'Santler Light Car', powered by a four-cylinder engine and priced at £165 for the two-seater model, £180 for a four-seater tourer and £130 for a special 'Tradesman's Light Delivery Car'. In an oversight, the written brochure for the model stated that the factory were already 'engaged' in the design of yet another motor car, which would be produced in order to rival the 'cheap American car in price and yet be throughout of the highest grade of workmanship'. It has to be said that the advertising and marketing executives today would certainly not inform prospective buyers that a better model was already in the planning stages, and thus risk sales of the current model; this, however, proved to be immaterial due to the onset of war. Late in 1914 the brothers registered the business as a Limited Liability Company, with themselves as directors.

By the end of hostilities the Santler Light Car was still available, though it is widely accepted that probably no more than a dozen or so were ever produced. As the early 1920s dawned, the Santler brothers made their final attempt at car production, and it is at this time that the name of another motor manufacturer was becoming prominent: the Morgan Motor Company, located just a few hundred yards from the Santler brothers' 'Malvernia Works' on the same Malvern road. One is left pondering the question why such innovative and skilled engineers as Charles and Walter therefore decided to produce a three-wheeled cycle car that was almost a copy of the local Morgan example. The Santler model was named the 'Rushabout', not too dissimilar from the name given to the Morgan offering, the 'Runabout'. Few of the Santler Rushabout vehicles were produced, and of those, some took the form of a delivery van and were purchased by local tradesmen. The initial price of £165 for the Santler version was reduced to just £85 in an attempt to undercut the Morgan rival, though this sales tactic failed as the Morgan gained in popularity. By the mid-1920s the Santler business had closed, though it is unclear as to why because despite flagging sales of its three-wheeled cycle car, the brothers did continue their other business activities: general engineering, repairs and electrical installations.

Walter moved to the north of England, where he found work as the resident engineer at Ampleforth College, North Yorkshire, and Charles moved to New Zealand, where he became a supervisor, installing electrical signalling on the railways. Charles later returned to his hometown and died in 1940 as the result of injuries sustained from the only bomb to be dropped on Worcester during the Second World War. He was seventy-eight and was believed to be carrying out caretaking duties at the Dowty Mining factory in the St John's area of the city.

2

The Morgan Motor Company

It is by no means unusual for two motor car manufacturers to operate from the same large city, and there have been instances of this around the world; to find two pioneers of the UK motor industry operating from a quaint Midlands spa town, within a stone's throw of each other, was unique. The established engineering company owned by the Santler brothers, now credited with building the first UK motor car, were joined on the Worcester Road in Malvern Link by Morgan in the early part of the twentieth century.

Henry Frederick Stanley Morgan (known to family and friends as 'Harry') purchased Chestnut Villa in 1905, a house on the Worcester Road in Malvern Link. He built a commercial garage to the side of the house in order to cater for the local motor car owners. In addition to offering a repair service, the Morgan garage also became a dealership for Darracq, Wolseley, Siddeley and Rover cars.

Henry Morgan was educated at Stone House, Broadstairs, at Marlborough College and at the School of Practical Engineering at the Crystal Palace, south London. By 1901 Henry had become an apprentice to two highly respected railway engineers, William Dean and George Jackson Churchward of the GWR Works at Swindon. After completion of his apprenticeship, Henry briefly worked in the drawing office at the railway, before leaving the company in 1904. His close friend Leslie Bacon, who incidentally had also served an apprenticeship on the railway, became his business partner. Alfie Hales, a motor engineer from Birmingham, was appointed as foreman to oversee all work within the factory. In addition to the services offered to motorists at the Morgan garage, Henry was also running a small omnibus service around Malvern, and by 1906 had opened a second garage in nearby Worcester, though this branch of the Morgan business was to close after one year.

By 1909 Henry had put his engineering background to good use with the construction of his own design, a three-wheeler with tubular steel chassis and a 7-hp V-twin engine. Henry was assisted in the early construction process by Mr Stephenson-Peach, the engineering master at Malvern College, with much of the work on the prototype being carried out in the college workshop. There was a very good reaction to Henry's first design venture, so much so that he was of a mind to put his three-wheeled example into production. This decision obviously did not sit well with his business partner Leslie Bacon, who, it is said, considered this to be quite a risk in such early days of motoring. As a result Leslie decided to leave the business, though he and Henry did remain good friends for the remainder of their lives, despite their early business differences. Henry's new 'Cyclecar' was unveiled at the 1909 Motorcycle show held at Olympia, London. This was a single-seat model steered by a tiller, with engine options of either a 4-hp or 8-hp V-twin. This machine, named the 'Runabout', created plenty of interest but few were built; the most likely reasons are the lack of a two-seater option and the outdated tiller steering. Despite the lack of sales for the first Morgan, Henry did enter an example in the MCC London to Exeter Trial, with his performance winning him a gold medal; it was to be the first of many competitions for both Henry and the Morgan brand.

By 1910 the first two-seater Runabout had been constructed, this time with a steering wheel and canvas hood; this version was greeted with great admiration when it was unveiled at the Olympia show later that year. As a result of this car's success, an unlikely alliance was formed between Morgan and Harrods. An example of the Mk II Runabout appeared in the window as the famous London store became the first Morgan dealer. However, the alliance was short-lived as Harrods wanted their own bodies fitted to the Morgan chassis; these bodies proved to be simply too heavy and were said to adversely affect the car's handling. Henry decided to terminate the Morgan-Harrods agreement, and soon established a network of Morgan dealers around the UK. In spite of the Runabout's success, Henry and the factory continued to work on other design ideas, and one of these included a four-seater Morgan which was used by the Morgan family. The Runabout continued with great success and the production volume was increased at the Worcester Road site. The vehicle was gaining great fame due to the high standard of its build quality and, more importantly, reliability. It featured a two-speed transmission (no reverse) with V-twin engines by JAP, though other engines could be, and were, fitted. By 1912 the Morgan Motor Company had been formed as a private limited company, having Henry as the managing director and his father, the Reverend H. G. Morgan, as chairman. In June of the same year Henry married Hilda Ruth Day, the youngest daughter of the Reverend Archibald Day, Vicar of the St Mathias Church in Malvern Link.

From that first Morgan cyclecar in 1909 up to the outbreak of the First World War, Morgan cyclecars had achieved tremendous success in motorsport, securing ten British and World records, and had won twenty-four gold medals in reliability trials; in addition, several other notable victories were gained on the race tracks of the UK. One very rewarding win was recorded by a Morgan with driver Harry Martin at the wheel during the first International Cyclecar Race at Brooklands. Several weeks after that success, Henry Morgan won the Cyclecar Cup in the 1,100 cc class after travelling at 60 mph for a full hour at the Brooklands banked track in Surrey; his father H. G. Morgan was in attendance on the day. Racing those early Morgans was very much a family affair, as Henry Morgan's sister Dorothy was a regular entrant in reliability trials, with several class wins to her credit. One notable win came in 1913, on the Worcestershire hillclimb track at Shelsely Walsh, where she gained the fastest time for a three-wheeler, and by the end of the year the Morgan Runabout had gained more wins in reliability and speed trials than any other cyclecar. Another significant win during the early years was gained by W. G. McMinnies while taking part in the International Cyclecar Grand Prix at Amiens in France. He and his passenger Frank Thomas won that day against a very strong field of entrants, which included four-wheeled cars. McMinnies was the editor of the popular magazine *Cyclecar*, so his victory and the subsequent publicity within the publication was a terrific tonic for the Morgan brand. Production increased yet again at the Malvern factory due to the publicity generated by the motorsport wins, and it became obvious at the time that the small Worcester Road factory was not large enough to cope with the increased productivity. In 1913 the company purchased a small plot of land in Pickersleigh Road, just a quarter of a mile from their original premises. During the summer of 1914 two new workshops were constructed on the site. Further development on the new site was brought to an abrupt halt with the outbreak of the First World War, and the Morgan factory played its part in producing munitions for the war effort.

Shortly after hostilities ended, the 'new' works at Pickersleigh Road were extended and two new workshops built on the site; it was officially opened on 16 October 1919. Shortly after this opening, Peter Morgan was born, and he was to play a key part in the Morgan story in later years. One model of note to emerge soon after the war was a vehicle whose name had been inspired by a Morgan customer some years prior, the 'Aero'. Flying ace Captain Harry Ball of the RFC had purchased a special-bodied Morgan Grand Prix model, which he said was the 'nearest thing to flying without leaving the ground', but sadly Capt. Ball was shot down and killed soon after taking delivery of his car; thus, the Aero name was bestowed on the new model in honour of the great flying ace.

In the years after the First World War, the Morgan company cemented its reputation as a unique manufacturer of hand-built cars in low volume and continued with their success in motorsport. In December of 1949 Henry Morgan gave an interview to the *Light Car Magazine* in which he recounted some noteworthy events, a short section of which I have reproduced here:

In 1931 I brought out a model with three speeds and reverse, one chain and detachable wheels. Previously all models had had a simple two-chain drive giving two speeds. On the sporting side the Runabout continued to uphold its reputation, winning race after race, for example, at Brooklands. In 1930, driving a 1100cc J.A.P racer, Mrs. Gwenda Stewart (later Mrs. Douglas Hawkes) broke the Hour record at a speed of over 100mph. As the attempt was made at Montlhery (France), Mrs. Stewart could not claim 'The Light Car and Cyclecar' Cup.

The year 1935 marked the advent of a new model fitted with four four-cylinder 8hp and 10hp engines. This was the best all-round three-wheeler we had turned out and, with slight modifications, it is in production today. For some years, competition from light cars had been getting very severe, owing to the improved performances and low cost of these four-wheelers. Our output dropped, and to keep the works busy, I decided to produce a small four-wheeler, light in weight with plenty of power. I had already experimented with various types. One of the first (in 1914) was fitted with a Dorman four-cylinder engine. Taking the successful four-cylinder, three-wheeler as the basis of design, I produced the four-wheeled models first shown in 1936 at the Paris Olympia Show. It was called the 4/4.

Looking back through the years, seeing both errors and triumphs in their correct perspective, I feel I have enjoyed it all; the motor trade has been – so far as I am concerned – a most interesting business.

Henry 'Harry' Morgan remained as chairman of the Morgan Motor Company until his death in 1959, at which time his son Peter took over the running of the factory. Peter continued the tradition of building hand-crafted cars, introduced several new models and became highly respected by everyone connected with the Pickersleigh Road works. When Peter passed away in 2003, he was succeeded by the first non-Morgan family member in the company's history, Mr Alan Garnett. This, however, was a short tenure of the company hot seat as Mr Garnett was replaced by a four-man management team consisting of Matthew Parkin, Tim Whitworth, Steve Morris and Charles Morgan (Peter's son). By 2010 Mr Parkin had left the company, and in 2013 Charles Morgan had also departed from his daily involvement with the factory, though he remains a major shareholder. At the present time Mr Morris is the company figurehead though other Morgan family members remain on the board.

Within the confines of a publication such as this it would be impossible to give a detailed account of every Morgan car produced over the years, so I offer a 'time-line' listing here:

1909: First Morgan three-wheeler exhibited at Olympia, London.

1910: Two-seater Runabout constructed.

1936: First four-wheeled production Morgan.

1938: Drop Head Coupe introduced.

1939–45: Pickersleigh Road factory used to produce goods for the war effort.

1945: Production resumes at the factory.

1949: Prototype produced using a 1.8 litre Vanguard engine.

1950: That prototype became the Plus Four, with engine now increased to the 2,088 cc unit. The company also made the decision in this year to bring to an end production of the three-wheeler.

1953: Modifications made to the frontal appearance of the Morgan with sloping radiator and headlamps now incorporated into the wings, a design which has lasted up to the present day.

1955: The 4/4 model reintroduced as the Series Two and was fitted with the Ford 100E 1,122 cc engine.

1956: Plus Four model has engine changed from the Triumph TR2 unit to the 100 bhp engine, as fitted to the TR3.

1960: The 4/4 Series Three launched, now fitted with the Ford 105E unit as fitted to the Anglia.

1961: The Plus 4 Super Sports launched, fitted with a tuned Triumph TR engine. The 4/4 Series Three now replaced by a Series Four, using the Ford 109E 1,340 cc engine.

1962: Historic racing achievement for Morgan this year as a Plus 4 Super Sports model driven by Chris Lawrence and Richard Shephard-Baron won the 2-litre class at the famous Le Mans 24 hour race.

1963: A 4/4 Series Five launched and fitted with a Ford 116E engine (1,498cc). The Plus 4 Plus unveiled at the '63 Earls Court Motor Show. The model featured a glass fibre body and engine from the Triumph TR4 sports car. This model was to cease production after a couple of years, as less than thirty examples were built.

1966: Legendary Morgan figure Mr Maurice Owen joined the company and was to oversee the development of the forthcoming Plus 8 model.

1968: At the Earls Court Motor Show of this year the Plus 8 is launched. Engine was the Rover V8 (3,529 cc). The 4/4 Series Five model was to become the 4/4 1600, as it was fitted with the Ford 1,599 cc unit; a 1600GT variant was also made available.

1970: The 4/4 models now fitted with the 1600GT Ford engine.

1975: The company offer a Plus 8 Sports Lightweight model, though fewer than twenty were built.

1976: The Rover SDI engine now fitted to the Plus 8, with the addition of a five-speed gearbox.

1981: A 4/4 Twin Cam model launched and fitted with the Fiat 1600 twin cam engine.

1982: The 4/4 model to be fitted with the Ford CVH engine (1,597 cc) as used in the hugely popular XR3 Escort.

1985: A re-launch for the Plus 4 model, now fitted with the Fiat 2-litre twin cam fuel injected engine and five-speed gearbox.

1988: A Plus 4 M16 model introduced and fitted with the Rover 3.9-litre unit, as fitted in the Range Rover Vogue SE.

1991: Plus 4 model now fitted with the Ford 1,600 cc fuel-injected engine. The model is also given the slightly wider chassis of the Plus 8.

1997: A 4.6-litre engine becomes an option for buyers of the Plus 8.

1999: The four-seater version of the 4/4 gets a re-launch and now comes fitted with rear bucket seats in place of the bench seat.

2000: The Morgan Aero 8 is unveiled at the Geneva Motor Show. Power came via the BMW 4.4-litre V8 unit.

2002: The Aero 8 GT (N) race car launched at the Autosport International Show. Special edition 'Le Mans 62' models launched and available in Plus 8 and 4/4 options. Just forty of each model built. Morgan made a return to the Le Mans 24 hour race with the De Walt/RSS Aero GT (N). The car had engine failure at two-thirds race distance.

2003: An entry-level model is launched by the company entitled the 'Runabout'. Only available in three colour options and standard specification, no options. Price was £22,000. To celebrate thirty-five years of production of the Plus 8 model, a special anniversary edition is announced; in the region of 200 were sold. A limited edition Aero GT Coupe announced.

2004: A very busy year. An Aero 8 model with USA specification was unveiled at the Los Angeles Motor Show. Due to the demise of the legendary Rover V8 engine, the final Plus 8 examples were produced after thirty-six years. This had been Morgan's best-selling model with around 6,000 produced. The Morgan name returns once more to Le Mans, but despite finishing the gruelling race, the Aero 8 did not manage to complete enough laps. The 'economy' Runabout ceased production. The Morgan Roadster is launched at the UK Motor Show, and intended as the replacement for the Plus 8. Power came from Ford's 3-litre V6 engine. A lightweight variant of the Roadster is also introduced, designed primarily as a track car. The Plus 4 gets yet another re-launch, this time fitted with the 2-litre Ford Duratec unit.

2005: A Morgan Roadster is announced, aimed at the North American market, with a little over eighty available. The Morgan Aeromax is commissioned by Prince Eric I. Sturdza, the President of Banque Baring Brothers Suisse.

The Morgan 'LifeCar' project announced a model to demonstrate that a high performance sports car with fuel cell power is possible.

2006: A special 70th anniversary edition of the 4/4 is announced. 142 examples produced, two for every year of production. A new version of the Aero 8 launched, with re-styled front end. New four-seater announced with a myriad of options available, including a choice of engines.

2008: A Morgan 4/4 Sport model launched, and after seventy-two years of production for the 4/4, this achieved a world record for a continuous production run. Aeromax production commences, two years after it made its debut at the Geneva Autoshow. An automatic gearbox is offered for the first time in a production Morgan.

2009: Morgan's centenary year. The company launch the SuperSport Junior pedal car, a two-thirds scale replica, designed to appeal to both collectors and to Morgan customers for their children. The pedal cars were built in the factory, alongside real cars. Aero SuperSports announced, and to have 4.8lt BMW V8 power. Aero 8 production ceased at the end of the year.

2010: The Roadster Sport model unveiled at the Geneva Motor Show. The Eva GT model announced at the Pebble Beach Concours d'elegance, California. A limited production of 100 examples. The legendary Morgan three-wheeler makes a return to production, was the announcement in November. The first cars/cyclecars delivered to customers in 2011.

The future: Despite an estimated production number of just 300 examples for the Morgan three-wheeler, the 1,000th example has since rolled out of the factory, with orders continuing to come in. The company unveiled a Morgan Electric Plus E car at the 2014 Geneva Motor Show in order to gauge potential sales. The car was developed with the aid of electric sportscar technology specialists Zytec and Radshape. The fuel cell concept car given the name 'LIFEcar' is to go into production, but now with a 'series hybrid drivetrain'. Capable of a 1000 mile range and weighing less than 800kg, the car has been developed with the assistance of the universities of Birmingham, Oxford and Cranfield. The Morgan Motor Company expands its markets into the UAE and China.

he rear of the Santler brother's factory in Merton Road, Malvern Link. This early publicity picture was used demonstrate cycles through the ages; the picture dates from the late 1890s.

his is the brochure picture of the Santler Rushabout in prototype form, a cyclecar which bears more than a assing resemblance to a similar Malvern Link product!

Here is another picture taken from the Santler brochure, this time showing the production version of their Rushabout; front- and rear-end body styling had obviously been altered by the time this model went into production.

Now recognised as the first car built in Britain, this is the Malvernia (also called the Santler Dogcart) after it was rescued from a blacksmith's yard, prior to its appearance in the Malvern Carnival.

Another Santler brochure picture, this time showing their 'Light Car', and dating from 1914; referred to in their brochure as 'The Rolls Royce of Light Cars', so were the Santler brothers the first to use this famous slogan?

The Santler brothers around 1901 with some of their staff, Charles at the wheel and Walter to the front of him the car was a 6 hp Santler which was registered in 1904. The picture, which shows sign writing on the factory wall, was most likely taken at the rear of their premises, which backed onto Merton Road.

This was the location of the first Santler workshops, now a block of apartments in the Quest Hills area, but once a series of brick and wooden buildings from where Thomas and Walter produced their early bicycles.

The frontage to these shops on the Worcester Road in Malvern Link is all that remains of the 'Malvernia Works', situated just a stone's throw along from the original Morgan factory site.

The final resting place of Charles Santler, in a hidden churchyard near to the junction of Madresfield and Malvern Link. Other Santler family members were also laid to rest in the same location.

This wonderful hand-painted mural, which clearly shows Malvern's proud connection with both Santler and Morgan, is on a shop wall in the centre of Malvern Link, on the corner of the Worcester Road and Pickersleigh Road.

The first Morgan garage/factory, which was located in Malvern Link; in later years the building's frontage wa
altered as Morgan stopped selling cars for others manufacturers and concentrated solely on their own models. I
the 1930s this site was sold to car dealers Bowman & Acock, and in more modern times it was a Ford dealershi

The site of the first Morgan factory as it looks today, and by coincidence it shares its fate with that of the earl
Santler workshops in the Quest Hills area around the corner; both were demolished to make way for apartments

This is an artist's impression of the 'new' Morgan factory at Pickersleigh Road, which appeared in a brochure dated 1925, and, despite the addition of further buildings in later years, the factory site looks much the same day as it did then, though a seventh building was later added to the six which appear in this picture.

Something of a time warp, the Morgan factory as it is today; employees from 100 years ago would have no trouble finding their way around even now, though the state-of-the-art Aero workshop might come as something of a shock!

An early advertisement for the Morgan Runabout three-wheeled cyclecar; this model established the Morgan brand as a market leader, with the advertisement clearly portraying this model's virtue of speed.

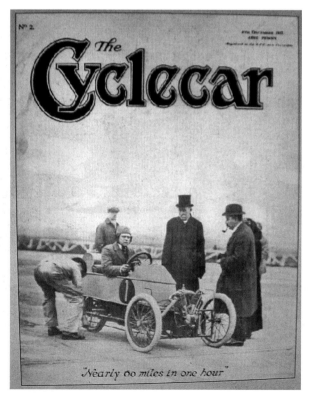

A fabulous cover from *The Cyclecar* magazine with Harry Morgan at the wheel of an early three-wheeler example at the Brooklands racetrack. Harry's father (in top hat) is a keen observer of the day.

Superb period publicity shot of new Morgan models; the picture was taken in Redland Road, Malvern Link, round the back of the original factory, a favourite location at the time for Morgan when it came to photographing new models. The road still exists, as do the houses.

The first 4.4 Morgan was released in 1936, and has been an extremely popular model with customers; the 4.4 remains an option to the present day and a modern version is seen here.

Early Morgan cyclecars were assembled in France under licence to R. Darmont, as this period (if somewhat faded) advertisement shows.

This was the 'new'-style Plus 4 Morgan, pictured at the factory in 1957.

The late Peter Morgan, son of company founder Harry Morgan, seen here in his own Morgan outside the factory frontage in Pickersleigh Road.

ne of the most famous racing Morgan cars of all time, affectionately known as 'TOK'; class winner at Le Man, e car still attracts crowds when brought out for various shows.

The roar of this modern Aero GT3 Le Man race car is a sound to behold. Morgan can boast a rich history i competition at the famous French circuit; this beast is aptly pictured nestling in the paddock at the histori Shelsley Walsh hillclimb track.

The company has a distinguished pedigree when it comes to motorsport, and their ARv6, seen here, is a serious track car, delivering 370 bhp. Based on the Morgan 3.7 Roadster chassis, the ARv6 has been stripped back and complemented with lightweight materials; it is the perfect companion for any serious track enthusiast.

Morgan cars are renowned the world over for being hand-crafted by a very skilled workforce and yet remaining up to date with the latest technology; this demonstrator Morgan was built partly without its outer bodywork in order to show clearly the construction methods used.

ove and overleaf: Morgan have produced many limited edition models over the years, all proving extremely
pular with loyal buyers; seen here is a recent release in the shape of the '100 year WR14 Edition +8 Speedster',
oduced to celebrate a hundred years of production at the Pickersleigh Road site.

The topic of greenhouse gasses and protecting the planet have been taken very seriously by motor manufacturers around the world; the Morgan Motor Company are no exception and have employed the considerable skills of their engineers and design team to produce an electric Morgan sports car for the twenty-first century.

A sketched portrait of Herbert Austin, from his later years.

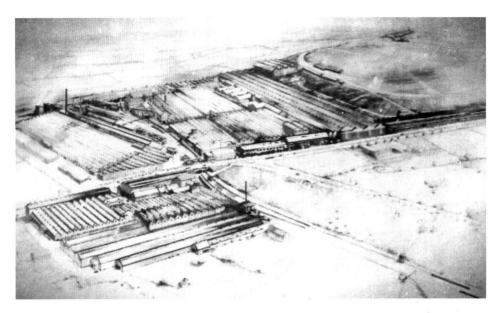

A sketch of the Austin factory at Longbridge; in addition to the main factory buildings, Herbert Austin created a whole village for his employees, including housing. The site went through several transformations, later becoming home to BMC, British Leyland and MG Rover.

The front view of Lickey Grange near Bromsgrove, home to Herbert Austin and his family for many years; the Austin 7 car was designed in the billiard room of this house by Austin and young engineer/designer Stanley Edge.

The rear view of Lickey Grange; the vast grounds surrounding the property have now been developed and houses built on the site. The main house still stands and has been converted into several luxury apartments.

The great Austin motor car industry was built upon the success of the little Austin 7 car, which still has a tremendous following among enthusiasts. This delightful early example is owned by Nick Turley.

The same Austin 7, as seen from another angle; simple engineering which really did bring motoring to the masses between two world wars.

The Austin 7 became very popular with fans of motorsport, from racetracks to hill climbs, and with many different body styles. Seen here is a sketch of an Austin 7 racer at speed. Many famous names from the world of motorsport cut their teeth with an Austin, including the late race car and team owner Bruce McClaren.

Many period magazine covers are now regarded as works of art in their own right; this photograph of the cover of *The Motor* publication from 1950 depicts a colourful artist's impression of the Austin A70 saloon.

Another cover from the same publication, this time featuring an Austin Somerset, and dated 1953. The company produced a series of cars which were given the name of English counties, such as Devon and Hereford; sadly there was no Worcestershire model, I suspect due to the length of the name.

3

Worcestershire and the Austin-Morris Connection

There are surely few counties in England that can boast to having such a plethora of legendary motor figures connected with them as Worcestershire, certainly within the world of motor manufacturing. The county would have been quite rightfully honoured just to have had motoring pioneers Henry Morgan and the Santler brothers' connection, but to have had two giants of UK motor manufacturing as a further affiliation was almost an embarrassment of riches. The names Austin and Morris will be forever etched into British motoring history as men who transformed motoring in the UK, in the beginning as individuals and later when their names were merged to form Austin-Morris, an iconic British brand. Worcestershire has a proud association with both men, as William Morris (later Lord Nuffield) was born in the city, and Herbert Austin (later 'Sir') made Worcestershire his home for over thirty years.

The William Morris link to the county might be considered a little tenuous, as he was simply born on the edge of the city in a terraced house in Comer Gardens and was moved away by his parents when he was only three years of age. Yet many a building in Britain has a (Civic Society) blue plaque adorning its frontage simply because a famous person was born there, died there, or just spent a very short time in residence. So I make no apology for including William Morris as a Worcestershire-born man, and of course there remains the mouth-watering prospect that had his parents not moved to Oxfordshire, it might well have been Worcestershire which became home to Morris Motor Cars. Herbert Austin, on the other hand, although not born in the county, did decide to make it his home for the last thirty-one years of his life and raised his three children in his adopted county.

My grandparents lived all their married life just around the corner from the birthplace of Lord Nuffield, and indeed when I first got married, my wife and I lived in the same road – just a few doors down from that famous terraced house – and yet it is only in recent years that I became aware of our proximity to the famous birthplace. It never fails to amaze me, the history that surrounds us all, often in our own towns and under our very noses, which we are blissfully unaware of. It is because I know the road and the birthplace of Lord Nuffield so well that I am left in awe of what this man achieved from such humble beginnings, though it would be folly to include the history of Morris cars within this title, as none of Morris's achievements can be attributed to his short life in Worcestershire. It was the county of his birth, nothing more.

Sir Herbert Austin, Lord Austin of Longbridge, 1866–1941

Herbert Austin, on the other hand, had a much greater association with the county, and despite the fact that he was not born in Worcestershire, he did spend the best part of his life in the county, and indeed set up the famous Longbridge Austin factory in North Worcestershire in 1905. Before any Birmingham residents complain about that last statement, I should point out that in geographical terms, Longbridge was a Worcestershire village at the time Herbert Austin built his factory there, but due to boundary changes which took place in 1919, Longbridge then became part of Birmingham.

Herbert Austin was educated in Yorkshire, and when the time came for young Austin to enter the workplace his father put him down for an apprenticeship on the Great Northern Railway; this, however, never came to pass as a meeting with his mother's brother was to change the course of his life. Austin's uncle had visited Australia during the 1880s, and it is believed that a young and adventurous Herbert Austin was captivated by the tales told to him by his uncle, and by the opportunities which lay in store in that country. By 1884 both Herbert and his uncle had decided that Australia was where their futures lay, and once there Herbert's uncle became the manager of an engineering company, with Herbert an employee. Within a couple of years Herbert had moved to another company in the same line of business, making parts for the Wolseley

Sheep Shearing Machine; the company had been set up by Frederick Wolseley, a Dublin immigrant. Through hard work, dedication and time spent at evening classes, Herbert was gaining something of a reputation as a very bright engineering student. By 1887 Herbert had met and married his Australian wife, Ellen Dron; by the following year he had been appointed manager of a small engineering company.

Frederick Wolseley, Herbert's employer, became ever more impressed with the contribution Herbert was making to the company, his attention to detail, engineering prowess and ability to spot faults with current designs and machinery. By 1893 Wolseley had moved his company to England, given Herbert shares in that company, and appointed him as factory manager. Sheep shearing machinery was certainly not in great demand in England, so Herbert began to explore other avenues in order to improve revenue for the company; by 1895 they worked making machine tools and various parts for bicycles. Herbert began to take an interest in the 'horseless carriage', which was gaining in popularity throughout Europe. It is believed that he became inspired by these new machines after a visit to the Paris Exhibition of 1894. Within a year he had built his very first 2-hp carriage, and by the mid-1890s Wolseley and his directors had agreed to invest around £2,000 in the manufacture of these new carriages, under the supervision of Herbert Austin. Within a couple of years, Herbert had built the second cyclecar (as they were becoming known), and by the turn of the century he had built the first Wolseley four-wheeled motor car, entering (and driving it) in the 1,000-mile trials of the Auto Club of Great Britain. Within a couple of years, though, Herbert Austin and the Wolseley company had parted after a disagreement over engine design/use, and Herbert purchased a disused printing factory at Longbridge, north Worcestershire. By December 1905 the Austin Motor Company Ltd was registered. The purchase price of the factory was said to be around £10,000, with around £20,000 working capital invested by Herbert, topped up with an investment by his old friend Frank Kayser, who had been the steel supplier to the Wolseley company. Later, Harvey Du Cros Jr (MD of Swift and the son of the chairman of the Dunlop tyre company) invested more funds, thus becoming a third director of the Austin company.

Over the next few years, car output increased along with a rapid rise in turnover; the number of employees was also to rise, and by 1913 there were nearly 300 staff at the Austin factory. During those early years, Herbert Austin and his family were living at Berwood Grove, a small Victorian mansion where Herbert had his study/drawing office, though he also had an office within the factory. With the increasing success of the factory and its products (Herbert referred to motor cars as a 'touring carriage'), Austin began to switch his designs from the popular open landaulet models to a closed limousine, and around the same time he became an early pioneer of setting up showrooms in order to display his vehicles. His showroom in the West End offered servicing, hire cars and the use of rooms. Herbert also looked to other ways of increasing productivity, and by 1908 had built a 100-hp sports car, begun to produce commercial vehicles, and can even take credit for being the first UK car manufacturer to build a 'motorhome', displaying it at the 1909 Olympia Motor Show.

The outbreak of war in 1914 was to put an end to car production, but the Longbridge factory was to play a vital role in the war effort. In the years 1914–18 the Austin factories produced several million shells, a large number of guns, around 2,000 aeroplanes and several hundred armoured vehicles; a huge number of lorries, ambulances and engines were also manufactured at the plant. The personal tragedy for Herbert Austin during the First World War was the death of his only son, Vernon, who was killed in France; Vernon had been an apprentice at the Austin factory. The company had begun 1914 with around 2,500 employees; by 1918 that figure had risen to 22,000, mostly women assisting with factory war work. At the time, the Longbridge factory complex was situated in a rural area which made travelling somewhat difficult for many staff; as result Herbert Austin purchased a 110 acre site (formerly a farm), and had cedar bungalows erected in which to house his extra workforce.

The fortunes of the Austin company, like many in the UK, took a downturn after the war and the company ran into financial problems; Austin's creditors stepped in. The bank brought in two men in order to rescue the business, R. F. Engelbach and Ernest L. Payton. Herbert Austin was also to lose his old friend Frank Kayser at this time due to re-organisation within the boardroom. Mr Engelbach assumed a role overseeing all production within the factory, and Mr Payton was entrusted to deal with all the finances. By 1910 Herbert Austin had moved into a large country house called Lickey Grange, which had a 200 acre estate attached to it. This was to be his sanctuary during those dark days of financial problems with the business and two men now basically operating his company, though he and his wife did still own half of the voting shares. Austin was a man of great resolve and determination, and in order to bring success back to his company he came up with the idea of building a small car for those at that time who were buying the very popular motorcycle and sidecar combinations. Herbert Austin took into his confidence an eighteen-year-old draughtsman by the name of Stanley Edge, and installed young Stanley in the lodge on the estate so that the pair could work in private on Austin's new concept. Legend has it that the new car, which was to be the now famous Austin 7, was designed in the billiard room of Lickey Grange and the prototype constructed in secrecy in a corner of the Longbridge factory. The official launch of the baby Austin car took place at Coleridge's Hotel in the summer of 1922, and was exhibited to the general public at the November motor show of the same year. Herbert Austin very wisely took out a patent on some of the car's features, thus ensuring that he was paid a royalty for every single Austin 7 produced; pretty sound business sense for a great engineer.

The car became a big success, not only in the commercial sense but also in racing circles, where it excelled, winning many class records. The sales figures really did speak for themselves, because in the first full year of production, 2,500 were sold, and this was to rise to 26,000 by 1929. The larger Austin Twelve motor car also enjoyed some good sales during that period, and between them the two Austin models in fact represented around a quarter of the total British output of privately registered cars from the late 1920s onwards.

As early as the mid-1920s there had been talk of mergers between several UK car makers, with one such proposal coming from Dudley Docker of Vickers that Austin, Morris and Wolseley should consider a merger. This came to nothing, as did Austin's attempt to affiliate the company with General Motors in America, or his suggestion to Henry Ford that the two companies might 'collaborate' in the British market.

Having played such a leading part during the First World War, with the manufacture of so many vital components of war, the Austin factory, and Herbert in particular, were once again called upon by government in 1936 to prepare for hostilities with Germany within a couple of years. Austin became the chairman of the Shadow Aero Engine Committee, with a brief to organise the production of a substantial number of Bristol aero engines. In the same year, Herbert Austin became Baron Austin of Longbridge. The year 1938 became quite significant in the history of the Austin Motor Company, as Herbert Austin (by now an elderly man) took the decision to recruit Leonard Lord. Within a short period Lord was taking many of the major decisions, which Austin seemingly allowed him to do more and more, including the introduction of two new models. Leonard Lord had clearly become Herbert Austin's successor, and at a dinner held in the winter of 1939 Lord is believed to have told Austin, 'You'll need a couple of coaches to take them away before I've finished,' referring to many of the more elderly and senior figures at the company; Lord's intentions were clear. Very soon after the war began, Herbert Austin was forced to resign from his post as chairman of the Shadow Aero Engine Committee due to ill health, namely exhaustion. During the winter of 1940 Austin was diagnosed as suffering from pneumonia; he died in May of 1941. Respectful employees of the Austin factory lined the nearby streets as the funeral cortège passed along; Austin is buried in the graveyard of Lickey church, Worcestershire.

Posts and titles held by Sir Herbert Austin:

1912: President of the Institute of British Carriage and Automobile Manufacturers.

1917: Knight of the British Empire and a Commander of the Order of Leopold II for his services during the war.

1918: Member of the Institute of Mechanical Engineers.

1919–25: Unionist Member of Parliament for the King's Norton Division of Birmingham.

1931: President of the Institute of Automobile Engineers.

1932: President of the Institute of Production Engineers.

1932: Chairman of the Birmingham General Hospital.

1932: Chairman of the Greater Birmingham Employment Committee.

1933: Appointed Justice of the Peace for Birmingham.

1934: President of the Society of Motor Manufacturers and Traders.

1934: Master of the Worshipful Company of Coach and Coach Harness Makers.

1936: Created Baron, Lord Austin of Longbridge.

1937: Honorary Doctor of Law bestowed upon him by the University of Birmingham.

1937–40: Chairman of the Shadow Aero Engine Committee.

1937: Member of the Livery of the Worshipful Company of Car Men.

1937: Honorary Member of the Institute of British Foundrymen.

1938: Elected Honorary Life Member of the Institute of Mechanical Engineers.

1939: President of the British Cast Iron Research Association.

1940: President of the Birmingham United Hospital and Governor of the Royal Cancer Hospital, London.

Life Member of the Court of Governors of the University of Birmingham.
President of the Motor Trade Association.

4

Shelsley Walsh Hillclimb Circuit

The rolling Worcestershire countryside is probably the last place one would expect to find the world's oldest motorsport venue, yet that is precisely what lies to the north-west of Worcester city centre, nestling beside the River Teme off the B4204. A former bridle path located on a farm, this famous hillclimb track has been in continuous use since 1905, with racing halted only by two world wars. The tough winding track has been driven by the great and good of motorsport history and includes names such as Stirling Moss, Peter Collins, Hans Stuch, Raymond Mays, Whitney Straight, Tony Marsh and a very young Alec Issigonis, later to become a legendary car designer.

My first encounter with Shelsley came when I was just entering my teenage years, and that initial smell of fuel and oil, coupled with the almighty roar of the powerful competition cars left a lasting impression upon me, and was responsible for my lifelong enthusiasm for motorsport. The other abiding memory for me was that the track and its surroundings did appear to be from another era, almost a place which time had forgotten, and it was only upon reaching manhood that I came to realise that this was exactly the magic which had captivated so many spectators throughout its long history. It is the oldest motorsport venue in the world, and predates more famous tracks such as Monza in Italy or the mighty oval Indianapolis circuit. But even more incredible is that the track and its surroundings have remained almost unchanged since its inception; it is quite literally a time warp, and one half expects Jeeves and Wooster to come walking out from behind a paddock building.

This unique venue owes its success to the Midland Automobile Club (MAC), a club founded in 1901 in Birmingham, which could boast a young Herbert Austin as one of its inaugural members. Formed principally to organise social gatherings, it was hardly surprising that someone would want to hold motoring competitions, and a hillclimb took place in October of 1901 at Gorcott Hill. Enthusiasm grew within the club for more similar events and over the next couple of years Weatheroak Hill, Edge Hill and Sun Rising Hill were used, but after problems with the police (speed limits on public roads) the club members decided that private land was required. One of the club's members, Mr Montagu Taylor, a farmer from the Teme Valley in Worcestershire, had a suitable bridle path on a steep climb located on his land; it was deemed suitable by club members, who quickly set about widening the bridle path, erecting fencing and laying down gravel over the earth surface. It was on 12 August 1905 that the very first competitive runs were made up the new track at Shelsley, with close to forty cars taking place. The inaugural event was a huge success, and after this an annual Shelsley hillclimb was arranged which took place up to the outbreak of the First World War. During those early years some very notable names appeared on the entry lists, some already well known at the time, and others who would make their mark on British motoring in the years ahead, names such as Victor Riley, W. O. Bentley and a certain cyclecar maker from Malvern, H. F. S. Morgan.

The Shelsley track was left idle during the war years, and it was 1920 before the roar of powerful engines was once more heard around the Teme Valley. The track had obviously by that time fallen into a state of disrepair, but the Midland Automobile Club brought in a steam roller in order to make sure that the surface was compacted and flat for the return to competition. Taking part in that first post-First World War event was a Mr Tony Vandervell, who many years later would build his own Vandervell Grand Prix cars, which took part in the World Championships. That 1920 event was a turning point in the history of Shelsley Hillclimb; firstly, stewards from the Automobile Association were used to man the car parking for spectators, bringing an orderly manner to the gathering, and secondly, it was also to be one of the last 'free' entry meetings for spectators. Leslie Wilson was drafted in by the club to oversee finances as the meetings had been running up huge losses, despite high entry fees for drivers. One of his first duties was to implement a charge (for male spectators) in order to ease the financial burden on club resources. By 1922 the hillclimb had become a very popular motorsport attraction, and it was believed that around 7,000 spectators were present, with somewhere in the region of 2,000 cars in the car parks surrounding the farm venue. Shelsley had become a major motorsport venue in the UK by this time and, reacting to accidents that had resulted in spectator injury at other race meetings, the Midland Automobile Club made improvements to Shelsley for the 1925 meeting. This is when the venue was given its well-known feature of right-hand side spectator terracing, with many trees felled; it still retains pretty much this layout today. The big attraction for that 1925 event was racing driver (and later speed record holder) Henry Segrave, already a Grand Prix winner at the French race of 1923.

By 1930, Shelsley had been chosen to host the British round of the World Hillclimb Championship, and in keeping with modern track surfaces, the Shelsley hill was better prepared with what resembled a tar macadam finish for better grip. The entries for that year included a brilliantly gifted hillclimb racer, the Austrian Hans Stuck, together with the legendary race car driver Rudi Caracciola in a 7.1-litre SSK Mercedes.

At this point in Shelsley's history, it is only fitting to mention a legend associated with the famous hillclimb circuit, one Raymond Mays. A racing driver for thirty years, Mays competed in various forms of motorsport from speed trials to hillclimbing and even Grand Prix racing. Raymond Mays became a firm favourite with the Shelsley crowd over the years stretching from 1923 through to 1950, when he retired from racing. He set the BTD (Best Time of the Day) up the winding Worcestershire track on an astonishing twenty-one occasions, and was crowned British Hillclimb Champion in its first two years, 1947 and 1948. Mays enjoyed further success after his retirement from active driving, when he became a leading figure in the BRM Grand Prix team.

As already stated, the great and good of world motorsport have graced the Shelsely track over the years, and not all of these were males. Many women have enjoyed enormous success racing against the clock at the world's oldest motorsport venue, and few were better than Kay Petre. Born in Canada in 1903, Kay moved to the UK in her twenties and married Englishman Henry Petre in 1929. She quickly developed a love of motorsport, and despite her diminutive figure (just 4 feet 10 inches tall) she could certainly handle some very fast and heavy machinery; she became a racing sensation throughout the 1930s. The three prominent motorsport venues in the UK at that time were Brooklands, Shelsley Walsh and Donnington Park; she was to achieve lap records at two out of the three during her career. She achieved her first lap record at Brooklands in 1934 driving a Bugatti at 124 mph, and then a second driving a Delage at 129 mph. Kay took her first Shelsley hill record in September 1935 driving Raymond Mays's old Riley, recording a time of 43.8 seconds. That same year she set yet another lap record at Brooklands, again in the Delage, this time at a speed of 134.75 mph. Having joined the Austin Works Team, Kay returned to Shelsley in 1937 driving a supercharged Austin 7 single seater and took 0.02 seconds off her previous track record.

One of Kay's other notable achievements was finishing the demanding Le Mans 24 Hour race in 1934 with her co-driver Dorothy Champney in a Riley Ulster Imp; the pair finished thirteenth. During that same year Kay Petre took part in three Grand Prix with her Riley, competing against many famous drivers, including Bernd Rosemeyer in his Auto Union. Her best placing was sixth in the Grosvenor Grand Prix at Cape Town, South Africa. Her career came to a premature end during a race at Brooklands in September 1937, while driving for the Austin team. It was during the 500 mile race that Reg Parnell is said to have made a mistake while overtaking another driver, hitting the banking before hitting the Austin driven by Kay; she sustained terrible injuries, but survived. After the accident she became a motoring journalist and passed away in 1994 at the age of ninety-one.

At the height of its fame, the Shelsley track was sharing the honours with the likes of Brooklands as one of the premier motorsport venues in Britain, and by 1932 the BBC aired a commentary from the venue lasting one hour and twenty minutes on both national radio and the 'Empire Service'. This made Shelsley the venue for the very first motorsport event to be covered on the air, and it was the venue for the first ever broadcast by a young Murray Walker, whose name was to become synonymous with motorsport commentary for many years.

Two meetings were planned for 1939, but with the outbreak of war only one took place before Shelsley Walsh once again fell silent. Once peace was declared, a group of Midland Automobile officials made a visit to the venue, only to find that five years of neglect had taken their toll, with nature having taken over. Undaunted, the club set about clearance and preparation works in readiness for a meeting in 1946 and labourers for the clean-up operation included some German prisoners of war who had been kept on the estate. The hard work did, however, pay off as clearly post-war motorsport fans were eager to see some action; one estimate put that 1946 spectator figure at around 14,000, with an entry of 117 cars.

By 1947 the RAC, the governing body of UK motorsport, introduced the first official British Hillclimb Championship, which was to consist of five rounds; Shelsley hosted its round of that championship in June, on a very wet track. That year was to see the appearance of a famous name of the future, John Cooper, using cars for the first time that he had built himself for the 500 cc class. Another famous name of the future took part in the September 1948 meeting, driving his Cooper 500 cc; that nineteen-year-old young man was S. C. Moss. Stirling Moss was fast making a name for himself in motorsport and that day at Shelsley he won the 500 cc class, setting a new 500 cc record. Many years later, Sir Stirling Moss said about the venue: 'Shelsley represented an important stage in my motor racing education; it demands real discipline, focus and concentration, qualities which matter to a Grand Prix driver.'

By the 1950s motorsport fans were favouring circuit style racing over hillclimbing, and attendance figures began to fall, not only at Shelsely, but at other such venues around the UK. By this time, the Grand Prix World Championship had been introduced, and this format of racing, at circuits such as Silverstone, was seen as more entertaining to the fee paying spectator, leaving the hillclimb venues with just a hard core of enthusiasts. This is not to say that Shelsely, along with other similar tracks, didn't manage to attract large crowds with the growing number of racing circuits in the UK, because it did, just not on the scale seen during its heydays of the 1920s, 30s and 40s. The British Hillclimb Championship remains an extremely popular arm of British motorsport, where cars and drivers remain accessible to the crowds, and admission prices are reasonable in comparison with some forms of motorsport. Shelsley Walsh on a race weekend is still an exciting place to be, with a fabulous atmosphere and the ghosts of racing's past greats all around. What makes Shelsley so special is that it has not lost its identity, like some British motorsport venues; the layout remains the same, as does the old paddock, the ascending track follows the same lines with the same famous corners and bends, and all cars start from the same start line as legends like Stirling Moss, Raymond Mays and Hans Stuck. It is a venue with a magical past, and thankfully has a bright future.

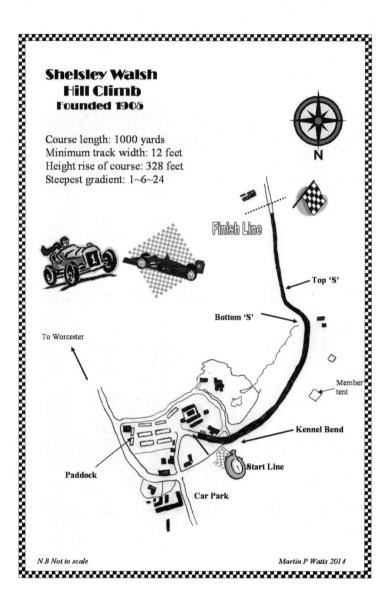

Plan of the Shelsley hillclimb track (not to scale).

This is a direction sign to Shelsley which is a nice period collector's item; it now adorns the wall inside the bar, with many other items of motorsport memorabilia.

Walls inside the club bar are certainly worth viewing; this wonderful montage of old racers really gives a flavour of the history surrounding this venue.

ere are few motorsport venues in the world which can match the charm and the feel of Shelsley, as little has anged in over a century; the covered parking bays in the paddock are a case in point.

The paddock has housed some of the greatest cars in motorsport history, including ex-Grand Prix machine
cars from the world of touring and rallying, and of course many hillclimb specials; a GT3 Morgan Aero is
pictured here.

view of the paddock area looking toward the start line.

This is the start line area at Shelsley; note the white line and rubber left on the tarmac as competitors warm their tyres in preparation for a fast start.

ront view of the start line, with vehicle being held in position by the marshal with his wooden chock under e tyre; the vehicle in this picture is a modern 3-wheeler Morgan.

Surely one of the most picturesque scenes in British motorsport, a view of the bottom 'S' bottom looking across the Teme Valley; a truly wondrous sight on a hot summer's day with the sound of cars racing against the clock.

A close-up shot of the same bends, with the start line and paddock just visible at the bottom of the hill.

This is the track just after the bottom bends, a favourite vantage point for many, and I make no apologies for having a Morgan in shot; this is after all a book about Worcestershire!

an out from the previous shot of the track, and you have this view of a car approaching the top 'S' bend ection. This view is from the spectator seating area, and the footpath up the hill can be seen to the right.

Close-up view of the 'S' section near the top showing not only the gradient of the hill, but also the steep grass covered banks at the edge of the track.

This is the view of the hill from the visitors' car park, a scene unchanged for many years.

Vox Villa is the famous commentary position at Shelsley Walsh; a young Murray Walker once graced its confines, and still returns occasionally for the odd meeting.

Some of the original farm buildings near the paddock, which includes a restaurant/café; the Morgan Motor Company hospitality unit is pictured here as they were hosting one of their excellent 'Thrill on The Hill' track days.

It is possible to get a really good idea of the gradient at Shelsley from this picture, with the steepness of the hil clearly visible in the background.

Perfect ingredients for a British summer's day; hot weather, time spent at an historic motorsport venue, and a vintage 3-wheeler Morgan (JAP-powered) – sheer bliss.

The Collins family home at Shatterford, near Kidderminster. (Picture courtesy of Louise Collins-King Collection)

above: This is a modern sketch of the garage on Worcester Road, Kidderminster, which was run by Peter's father. His office was in the room at the front with the art deco bow window; the earlier Collins haulage business at Mustow Green was demolished some years ago and is now a car park.

right: This is a photograph of the cover of the Autosport publication from 1956; his gesture by Peter to give up his Lancia Ferrari for teammate Fangio earned him the respect of not only his team, but also the 'tifosi' Ferrari supporters. Theoretically Peter could still have won the World Championship himself at this point, and is quoted as saying that there was plenty of time for him to win as he was still young (twenty-four at the time).

SEPTEMBER 7, 1956

AUTOSPORT

1/6

EVERY FRIDAY

Vol 13   No. 10

BRITAIN'S MOTOR SPORTING WEEKLY

IN THIS ISSUE

GRAND PRIX OF EUROPE · FULL REPORT

DB3S / PETER COLLINS

By 1955 Peter had gained a reputation for being an excellent driver of sports cars and for competing in endurance races; collector's cards of the period would often portray famous racing drivers, and Peter is seen here at the wheel of the Aston Martin DB3S, competing at Goodwood.

Peter married American actress Louise King after a very short whirlwind courtship; the pair became inseparable, and Louise was quoted as saying many years later that they only spent one day apart in their eighteen months together. After the marriage they moved into a house in the grounds of the Ferrari estate at Marranello, Italy, later deciding to live on a yacht in the harbour of Monaco. (Picture courtesy of Louise Collins-King Collection)

GROSSER PREIS VON DEUTSCHLAND
NÜRBURGRING
3. AUGUST 1958

Veranstalter:
AvD
Automobilclub
von Deutschland

AUTOMOBIL·WELTMEISTERSCHAFT

This poster is advertising the German Grand Prix at the Nurburgring, 3 August 1958; it would be Peter's last race, as he was killed when battling for the lead in his Ferrari.

Peter and Louise's 1957 Ford Mercury estate car; so huge the couple would refer to it as the 'row of shops', the Ferrari badges on the side are a humorous addition. (Picture courtesy of Louise Collins-King Collection)

Above: Peter's funeral took place at Stone church, Kidderminster. A private family service was held before Peter was laid to rest in the churchyard; a public service of remembrance was held several days later, with hundreds packing the church and grounds.

Left: Peter's widow Louise kindly allowed me to use this picture of just some of the floral tributes from the service at Stone church.

IN MEMORY OF
PETER JOHN COLLINS
WHO DIED AUGUST 3, 1958
AGED 26 YEARS
WITH A CHEERFUL SMILE AND A
WAVE OF THE HAND HE JOURNEYED
INTO THE UNKNOWN LAND.

Peter's headstone in Stone churchyard. It is incredible to think what life he packed into those twenty-six years

The birthplace of Nigel Mansell, in the village of Baughton, near Upton-upon-Severn; Nigel was born in this house on 8 August 1953. Inset is a sketch of the house in the 1950s when the downstairs was a café run by Nigel's parents.

Silverstone 1991 and Nigel driving for the Williams team had a terrific battle with Senna all season. However Senna ran out of fuel on the last lap of the British Grand Prix and Nigel stopped to give him a lift back to the pits, much to the joy of the British fans. Senna in yellow helmet can just be seen, sitting on the side pod of Nigel's car.

Opposite page: A press release picture of Nigel in his Williams Renault attire, holding his famous Union Jack inspired helmet.

The area around the old Abbey curve and Farm Straight; standing in this position today one would see the hu[g]e modern pit complex opposite.

5

Peter Collins and Worcestershire's Grand Prix Connections

I have been an avid fan of Grand Prix racing since the 1960s, and I'm sure it was sitting in a gorgeous Austin Pathfinder pedal car during my first week at school which initially triggered this. Throughout my childhood it was those metal toy 'Dinky' racing cars which took pride of place in my bedroom, along with any boys' annuals which contained pictures and stories relating to Grand Prix adventures, and drivers such as Moss, Hawthorn, Hill (Graham and Phil), Fangio and the like. By the time I was given a magical contraption called the 'Viewfinder', containing circular colour slides of Jim Clark in his Lotus and Graham Hill driving the BRM, I was totally hooked on Formula 1 racing. It was probably around this time that I was taken along to my first hillclimb experience at nearby Shelsley Walsh, where at that time many ex-Grand Prix cars were taking part; it was like Christmas and my birthday all rolled into one.

Although I followed Grand Prix racing avidly through the 1970s and beyond, attending races and getting to meet many of my idols in the flesh, it would always be those dangerous, glory days of racing in the 1950s which I most favoured. Formula 1 racing remains a hugely dangerous sport, but thanks to improved safety features, the cars and circuits around the world now claim far fewer lives than in the past. Largely thanks to car design and barrier improvements, drivers are now able to survive some horrendous high-speed accidents, unlike their predecessors in the 1950s. Those courageous drivers of front-engined cars did not have flame retardant overalls, sophisticated helmets with neck supports, tightly fitting safety harnesses or the benefit of crash barriers all around the track. They would often race in plain linen overalls, or even a pair of casual trousers with a polo-neck shirt or even a woollen jumper, a conventional helmet with nothing more than a thin layer of cork as protection for their head, gloves as worn by most family car motorists of the day, and most certainly no form of seat belts. The obvious result was that in the event of a serious crash, there was every likelihood the driver would either be killed or at the very least sustain serious injury. The death rate in Grand Prix racing at that time was alarming, and yet, as the drivers witnessed their friends and fellow colleagues being killed at a frequent rate, they continued to battle and dice with each other at high speed and on dangerous circuits, gaining great respect and admiration from the fans who were lucky enough to have witnessed man against machine during one of the most exciting eras in motorsport.

For anyone with only a slight knowledge of motor racing history, names such as Moss, Hawthorn and Fangio spring immediately to mind when the 1950s Grand Prix era is mentioned; but it took more than a handful of famous drivers to make up the starting grid at these races. One such man was Peter Collins from Kidderminster, Worcestershire, the son of a garage owner; Peter would become one of the truly great stars of the 1950s Grand Prix scene, and a highly respected sports car driver.

Peter John Collins

Born 6 November 1931, Kidderminster, Worcestershire
Died 3 August 1958, Bonn, Germany

Peter was from Mustow Green, Kidderminster, the son of a local haulage contractor and garage proprietor (a Ford dealership on the Worcester Road). I spoke earlier of sitting in a vintage pedal car at school, and believing that it kick-started my lifelong enthusiasm for motor racing; I now know where I went wrong because Peter Collins also had a pedal car at a young age, to which his father fitted a small lawnmower engine, and no doubt this small taste of speed at such a young age was the spark which started the fire. As a natural progression, Peter became an apprentice at his father's garage upon leaving school, and in a very short space of time he turned his interest to motoring competitions. Peter began his racing exploits in a Cooper 500 Mk II single seater car, believed to have been a birthday gift from his parents, and in his first serious race, at

Brough in Yorkshire, he was placed eighth. It is understood that Austen May, a friend of Peter's father, was so impressed with Peter's skill and enthusiasm that he convinced Peter's father to purchase Stirling Moss' ex-Cooper Mk II car. By 1949 Peter was making an appearance at the Goodwood Easter meeting. By June of the same year, that Mk II Cooper was replaced with a Mk III Cooper and in July Peter was entered for the 100 mile race at Silverstone airfield track. Peter was mixing his racing experiences between circuits, trials and hillclimbs at this stage, including the Shelsley Walsh venue close to his home. Peter continued to have success in racing with wins at Goodwood and Castle Coombe. By 1951 Peter was beginning to really make a name for himself as a promising prospect for the future, with some team managers keeping a keen eye on his progress through the ranks.

Fate played a hand in the future of Peter Collins in 1951 in the form of a Worcestershire connection, when Kay Petre, the female track record holder at Shelsley Walsh, invited Peter to a party which she was hosting. It was at that party that Peter met the Aston Martin team boss, John Wyer, and persuaded him to give him a test drive in sports cars. His wish was granted, and Peter took part in tests at Silverstone for the Aston team. Also present that day at the track were the HWM Formula 2 racing team, and Peter ended the day with not one offer but two contracts, for Aston and HWM. Peter got off to an excellent start in sports car racing, taking victory at the Goodwood 9 Hours race, proof to anyone who needed it that Peter was an accomplished race driver in both single seaters and sports car endurance races. His career with HWM was not a great success as the car was under-powered, his best placement being sixth in the 1952 French race. Peter would be recruited by Tony Vandervell in 1954 to drive the 'Thinwall Special' in the Formula Libre class and carry out test drives for Vanwall. Despite a very promising beginning to his racing career, Peter had not enjoyed the immediate race success which he had hoped for, but all that was to change in 1955 when he was given a 'Works Team' drive in the 250F Maserati at the Italian Grand Prix. He was recommended to Enzo Ferrari by English driver Mike Hawthorn, and in 1956 he raced for the prancing horse team alongside the legendary Juan Fangio of Argentina. He enjoyed a magnificent debut season with the Ferrari team, and at still only twenty-three years of age showed a maturity beyond his years in his driving ability, skill and mechanical knowledge. He took two victories in 1956, at the demanding Belgian mountain circuit at Spa, and at the very fast track at Reims, and by the time the World

Championship arrived at Monza for the Italian Grand Prix, Peter was actually in with a good chance of winning the world title. What happened at that race has passed into motor racing folklore, and earned Peter the respect of so many people.

The race was the eighth and final round of the 1956 World Championship and consisted of fifty laps around the old Monza 10,000 km circuit with its high banked section. Coming into the final race, Peter Collins had an outside chance of clinching the world title as he lay just eight points behind his Ferrari teammate Fangio. The points scoring back in the 1950s was quite different to that of today, with only the five best performances of the season coming into the final equation. One must also consider that at that time it was possible to share points as one driver within a team could (or be asked to) surrender his car to a more senior team driver in the event of mechanical problems. Stirling Moss, driving the Maserati, was leading the race by half distance with Schell in the Vanwall close behind; the Ferrari team of Fangio, Collins and Musso were still in contention, though the fourth Ferrari driver, De Portago, had retired. The nineteenth lap was the turning point for both the race and for the 1956 World Championship, because as Moss came past the pits in first place, Fangio and his Ferrari were nowhere to be seen. Within seconds, Fangio's car came limping into the Ferrari pits with steering problems, came to a halt and Fangio exited the car. Fangio, the legendary Argentine driver, needed to finish the race, so it was a matter of which remaining Ferrari driver would be called upon to surrender their car to him; the crowd waited in anticipation. Meanwhile, a sharp shower of rain and a pitstop for Schell meant that Moss was now leading the Ferrari drivers Luigi Musso and Peter Collins. Musso was called into the pits for a tyre change, and everyone assumed that this was the point at which Musso would surrender his car to Fangio, who was waiting in the pits with his helmet on; after all, Musso was not in contention to win the championship. To the astonishment of everyone, Musso put the car into gear after the tyre change and accelerated away; there was no outburst of applause this time from the patriotic Italian crowd for a Ferrari leaving the pit lane, as was the normal custom. A couple of laps later, Peter Collins came into the pits, also for a tyre change, and upon seeing Fangio standing in the pits Peter duly offered the great man his car. In doing so he surrendered any chance of becoming world champion, though in hindsight he needed to win and set the fastest lap in order to acquire enough points to overtake Fangio and win his first championship, possible but unlikely given his race position at the time of his incredible gesture. Fangio gave Peter a pat on the back as he stepped into Peter's car and the crowd gave Peter an amazing ovation in recognition of what he had just done.

Stirling Moss went on to win the race, leaving Fangio and Collins to share three points each for second place, and those points were enough to clinch the World Championship for Juan Manuel Fangio and the Ferrari team. Asked later why he had made that incredible sporting gesture, Peter said that he was only young (twenty-four), and there would be plenty more opportunities for him to become champion; sadly that was not the case. That selfless act by Peter earned him the respect of Fangio and Enzo Ferrari, and endeared him greatly to the Ferrari fans. Fangio will always rank as one of the greatest drivers of all time, and he had this to say some years later about Peter Collins's gesture at the 1956 Italian Grand Prix: 'I was moved almost to tears by the gesture. Peter was one of the finest and greatest gentlemen I ever met in my racing career.' Fine praise from a motor racing legend.

For the 1957 season, Peter would be joined in the Ferrari team by his 'mon ami mate' Mike Hawthorn; the dashing blond English driver had become great friends with Peter since racing together at Goodwood some years earlier. They were tremendous friends, and would refer to each other as 'mon ami mate'; each enjoyed the company of young ladies, both had a great sense of humour and both loved a pint of beer at the local. The 1957 season was to prove a disappointing one, with Peter only finishing ninth in the championship, though the year did have brighter moments for the Worcestershire driver. Peter met American actress Louise King for a date at the Coconut Playhouse Bar in Miami, after which the pair became inseparable and married within a few weeks. Louise had starred in the Broadway production of *The Seven Year Itch* alongside actor Tom Ewell, who would eventually be cast in the film version of the play, which starred Marilyn Monroe, and indeed Louise had met Marilyn during the Broadway production. Previous published reports suggest that Peter's boss at the time, Enzo Ferrari, might have taken displeasure at the thought of his young English driver being distracted from his racing duties; in fact, Mr Ferrari and his wife Laura made Peter and Louise most welcome back in Italy and the couple were installed in an apartment over the Cavallino Restaurant, situated next to the Ferrari factory, later moving to a villa within the factory grounds.

For the 1958 racing season the Ferrari team pairing of Mike Hawthorn and Peter Collins had the new 246 Dino car, though Peter made a rather poor start to the season, and he and Louise had by that time moved to live on a yacht in the harbour at Monaco. The season continued to be a frustrating one for the Ferrari team when Luigi Musso was killed at the French Grand Prix at Reims and the pairing of Hawthorn and Collins failed to finish the classic Le Man 24 Hour race. Fortunes were to change for Peter and the Ferrari team on 19 July at the British Grand Prix, which took place at Silverstone. The Ferrari team enjoyed a one-two finish with Peter Collins winning the race and Mike Hawthorn finishing second; it was to be Peter's only win of that year. In his book, *Champion Year*, Mike Hawthorn stated that he, Peter and Louise enjoyed a drink in the beer tent after the race before Peter and Louise headed off in their car to Peter's parents' house at Kidderminster, taking Mike's sports jacket with them, which contained his keys, money and his beloved pipe! Mike further says that Peter and Louise had been looking for a house in his home town of Kidderminster for when he gave up racing, stating that they had found a Georgian house and left a deposit on it before heading back to their yacht in Monte Carlo, before heading to the Nürburgring for the German Grand Prix.

The old/original circuit at the Nürburgring in Germany was a notoriously difficult track to master for any driver; just one lap took over nine minutes to complete and covered a distance of over fourteen miles, in excess of 212 miles for the race itself. Due to the death of Ferrari driver Luigi Musso in France, Mike Hawthorn and Peter Collins were joined in the bright red cars by Wolfgang 'Taffy' von Trips. By lap ten of the race Peter Collins was in the lead, followed by teammate Mike Hawthorn (with a weak clutch) and then Tony Brooks in his Vanwall. By the following lap Tony Brooks had managed to pass both Mike and Peter. Mike was observing Peter from his close position in third place, believing that Peter and Tony were having so much of a duel for the lead that he was worried that they might touch each other; Mike was later to comment that he thought Peter was driving as well as he had ever seen him on that day in Germany. All three cars approached the bend before the Pflanzgarten corner, not a particularly fast bend, but according to Mike quite slippery, with a small bank on the outside and trees beyond. Tony Brooks was leading Peter's Ferrari by a couple of car lengths as they approached this bend, and Mike Hawthorn came right up behind Peter, but then Peter accelerated away. The best eyewitness account of exactly what happened next came from Peter's best friend and Ferrari teammate, Mike Hawthorn; I quote from Mike's book, *Champion Year*:

He went round the corner perfectly normally but running wide, and the car slid, drifting out. His back wheel hit the bank and the car lifted, running with the rear wheels on the bank which is about twelve inches high. God, I thought, the silly fool, we're both going to be involved in this. I thought he would spin off the bank across the road and I would hit him. I was just thinking up some choice words to say to him when we climbed out of the two bent Ferrari's when, without the slightest warning, fantastically quickly, his car just whipped straight over. It gave no indication that it would do this, it just turned over. I could not believe that it had happened; it came as a complete paralysing shock. There was a blur of blue as Pete was thrown out and I put the brakes on hard and almost stopped as I looked round. I saw the car bounce upside down in a great cloud of dust, before it came to rest.

Mike Hawthorn carried on, intending to stop at the scene of the crash on the next lap, but shortly after passing the pits he lost all drive in his Ferrari and it came to a halt; he had to remain in that position until the end of the race, when he was given a lift to the crash scene by an official. He arrived to find Peter's car upside down, with fencing broken and Peter's helmet beside the car, together with one shoe. He picked these items up and headed back to the pits, only to find that Peter's wife Louise had been driven to the local hospital by the Ferrari team boss, Tavoni. Returning to his hotel room to change out of his race overalls, Mike Hawthorn heard the news that his friend Peter had been taken to the hospital at Bonn by helicopter. Artur Keser of Mercedes drove Mike to the hospital at Bonn, after he had gone to Peter and Louise's room and packed their bags; they reached the hospital around 10.30 in the evening. Mike was given the news that Peter had died from the injuries which he sustained in the crash, and at that point his only thoughts were for Louise, and getting her away from the reporters and photographers who had already gathered at the hospital. Mike accompanied Louise back to London airport the next day, and then drove her up to Peter's parents' house in Kidderminster.

Mike Hawthorn not only lost his Ferrari teammate that day, but also his best friend, drinking pal and confidant; Peter's passing hit him very hard indeed. Peter's funeral was a private affair, at the request of his family, which took place a short distance from his parents' home, at St Mary's church, in the village of Stone near Kidderminster, and Peter was laid to rest in the churchyard. A memorial service for Peter was held on Sunday 10 August in order to give people the opportunity to pay their last respects; both the church at Stone and the grounds were packed with people, including racing drivers, and the service was relayed via loudspeaker to the crowd outside.

I have visited Peter's grave on several occasions over the years; it is a simple headstone which makes no mention of his racing exploits, and apart from his name and dates, a brief inscription reads: 'With a cheerful smile and wave of the hand he journeyed into the unknown land.' There is a stained-glass window within the church in memory of Peter; it reads: 'In memory of Peter John Collins 1931–58, God gave him courage and a cheerful heart.'

In addition to being a highly respected Grand Prix driver, Peter was an outstanding sports car driver, finishing second at the famous Le Mans 24 Hour race in 1955 in an Aston Martin DB35 with his partner Paul Frere. He also won the Sebring twelve-hour race in 1958, driving a Ferrari 250 TR58 alongside Phil Hill. His most famous sports car win came in 1955 in the Mercedes Benz 300 SLR when he partnered Stirling Moss around the gruelling Targo Floria mountain course in Sicily.

Peter's 'mon ami mate' Mike Hawthorn went on to win the 1958 World Championship but was killed on the morning of 22 January 1959 while driving his Jaguar on the A3 Guildford by-pass, losing control at high speed; no other vehicles were involved. It had been a tragic few months for those involved with the 1958 Ferrari Grand Prix team, with the death of Luigi Musso, Peter Collins, the chief Ferrari engineer Andrea Fraschetti (who was killed testing a 246 Dino at Modena), and then the World Champion Mike Hawthorn.

Peter's widow Louise initially resumed her acting career, touring in a successful play with Peter Ustinov, then later becoming a panel member on the TV show *What's My Line*. She also became a presenter on the American TV programme *Today* before turning her back on show business for a career in real estate, in both New York and Connecticut. Louise retired to Sarasota, Florida, in 1994 and now limits herself to just one major 'outing' a year; one such outing saw her at the Shelsley Walsh hillclimb for a Peter Collins Commemorative weekend.

Peter's V6 Ferrari 246 Dino, chassis number 002, made its race debut on 2 February 1958 in Buenos Aires, driven by Von Trips. On 4 May Peter drove the car to victory at the International Trophy meeting at Silverstone, later using the same car for Grand Prix at Monaco, Holland, Belgium and his last race win at the British Grand Prix at Silverstone. This was the car in which he was killed at the German Grand Prix at the Nurburgring; it's believed the car was either completely rebuilt or scrapped, and the serial number assigned to another chassis for the 1959 season. At the end of its racing time the car was broken up by the Ferrari factory and does not survive.

Worcestershire's Other Grand Prix Connections

Nigel Ernest James Mansell
Born August 1953, Baughton, Worcestershire
The county is fortunate to have had one of the all-time great Ferrari Grand Prix drivers as its residents, especially such a respected figure like Peter Collins, who always remained one of Enzo Ferrari's favourite drivers. But the Ferrari F1 connection does not end with Peter, because ex-World Formula One Champion Nigel Mansell was also born in the county, in the tiny village of Baughton, just outside Upton upon Severn, in August 1953. Nigel was born in a room above his parents' tea shop, his parents remaining in the village until Nigel was three years of age. The local public house across the road from Nigel's birthplace boasts that its car park was the scene of Nigel's first motoring exploits as he used to drive his pedal car around in front of the pub.

Due to Nigel's father working for British Aerospace, the family moved from Baughton to Hall Green, now classified as part of Birmingham, but once part of the Yardley Parish of Worcestershire! Like so many racing drivers in recent years, Nigel was to learn his basic skills in the sport of karting, on the tracks of both the UK and Europe. By the time he had come to the end of his teenage years, Nigel had won the British karting title, seven Midlands titles and one northern title. Nigel's next step on the ladder to become a world champion began when he made the move into Formula Ford single seater racing. By 1977 he had become the British Formula Ford Champion and made the step up to Formula 3 racing the following year. The big leap into Grand Prix racing came by 1980, when he joined Colin Chapman's Lotus team and made his debut at the Austrian Grand Prix. Nigel first came to my attention when I attended Silverstone to watch the British Grand Prix in 1983; he was driving the famous black and gold JPS and had qualified eighteenth on the grid. But it was not his race qualification which caught my eye that weekend, but the way he drove in the race itself, with a determination and focus; it was a sight to behold as he cut through the field lap after lap and eventually finished fourth.

Nigel continued to race for Lotus until 1985, when he joined the Williams team, where he achieved a great deal but still failed by the smallest of margins to become world champion. By 1989 he had become the first Worcestershire driver since Peter Collins to sign for the Ferrari team, and in fact was the last driver that Enzo Ferrari was to sign himself before his death. The Ferrari cars at this time were not as competitive as Nigel would have liked, and despite very limited success on the track and the odd displays of brilliance, it was to be a fruitless couple of years driving the famous red cars, though his grit, determination and effort did not go unnoticed by the *tifosi* (Ferrari fans), who called him '*il leone*' (the lion).

He decided to rejoin Frank Williams for the 1991 season and was given a very competitive car once more, but just failed once more to become champion. The highlight of that season for me, and many other F1 fans, was to see Nigel win the British Grand Prix at Silverstone, and I was lucky to be standing on the Abbey Curve when Ayrton Senna ran out of fuel on the last lap and was given a lift back to the pits on the side-pod of Nigel's Williams Renault. For Nigel and his adoring fans, 1992 was to be the year when it all came right and at long last he was crowned World Champion in F1. All those years of hardship which he and his devoted wife Rosanne had put themselves through, in the belief that one day Nigel would make it to the very top of world motorsport, had finally paid off. Then, having achieved his goal, Nigel needed a new challenge, and was to find this in the USA, signing a contract to drive for the Newman/Haas Indy CART team. This series, for want of a better explanation, is the equivalent of a Formula 1 season on American circuits, and the teams quite often include ex-Grand Prix drivers. To have the current F1 champion taking part in their American series was quite a coup for the organisers, and Nigel would not disappoint. In 1993 he became the CART champion at his first attempt, and as that racing season finished before the F1 season, it meant that he held both titles at the same time for a short period.

Nigel was to make a return to Grand Prix racing towards the end of the 1994 season, once more with Williams, but these were to be his last outings in a Williams car as he decided to join the McLaren team for 1994; it was a brief liaison, and after just two races Nigel made the decision to retire from the Grand Prix scene. Having lived in Port Erin on the Isle of Man throughout his Grand Prix career, Nigel purchased a golf club in the west of England, which he developed once he had hung up his helmet. He did make a brief return to motorsport on a few occasions, taking part in three races of the British Touring Car Championship in 1998 and the 2005 Race of Legends (for ex-F1 stars); he has also raced at Le Man, sharing a car with his two sons.

Motorsport titles: F1 World Champion 1992, CART Champion 1993
Honours: OBE, CBE
BBC Sports Personality of the Year, 1986 and 1992

Miscellanea

The Mitre Oak Public House
A typical English country pub situated on the A449 at Crossway Green, between Worcester and Kidderminster, is an unlikely venue to play a part in the motorsport history of Britain, yet this public house has two claims to fame within the sport. I was informed by a local resident that Grand Prix driver Peter Collins from Kidderminster used to frequent the pub with his pals during his Cooper 500 racing days. Peter and several friends would set off from the car park at the side of the pub and race each other along the fast dual carriageway into Worcester, through the city, and then out toward Malvern on the straight stretch of road which links the villages of Powick and Madresfield. There were of course far fewer vehicles on the roads at that time, certainly no speed cameras, and the long dual carriageway between Kidderminster and Worcester did not have the numerous speed restrictions and traffic calming measures it has today. No doubt Peter honed his racing skills on that section of road with its high-speed straights and sweeping bends, and he would be horrified to see what it looks like now.

The Mitre Oak lies a few miles from the Shelsley Walsh hillclimb track, and it was to this public house that some Shelsley racers retired in September 1947 after an enjoyable day at the track. Among that group of men was Maurice Googhegan, and they were discussing venues where they could race their cars circuit-style as Brooklands had just been sold and Donington was still full of ex-Second World War vehicles and plant. Maurice informed the group that near his home lay a disused airfield at Silverstone with some long runways, and he had tested his own car there the previous year. The airfield idea was met with agreement from the assembled group, so they agreed to make use of a two mile circuit which Maurice suggested for their first race. Around a dozen cars took part in that first Silverstone race, which has passed into motorsport folklore as the 'Mutton Grand Prix', due to the fact that during the race a driver collided with a grazing sheep which had wandered onto the track. Other incidents included a person being stabbed in the arm by a pitchfork left lying around, and a landing Tiger Moth plane almost clipped one of the race cars whilst landing! Within a couple of years regular races were being held at the ex-airfield, and Silverstone was established as the 'home of British motor racing', all thanks to a conversation which had taken place in a Worcestershire pub. Peter Collins, a Mitre Oak regular, went on to win the British Grand Prix at the Silverstone circuit, his last race win before being killed in Germany.

Richard John Beattie 'Dick' Seaman 1913–39

Englishman Dick Seaman raced for the legendary Silver Arrows Grand Prix team during the 1930s. He won the German Grand Prix in 1938, but was killed at the La Source hairpin at the Spa race track in Belgium the following year, when his car crashed and caught fire. Dick Seaman was badly injured and died a couple of days later in hospital. Those facts appear quite straightforward enough, but a legend has grown up surrounding the remains of his car, a story that I first saw reported in my local Worcester newspaper several years ago; it intrigued me intensely.

Dick Seaman's mother, Lilian Bettes-Seaman, had purchased a large country house for him (and his German wife) called Pull Court, close to Upton in Worcestershire. I have no idea where this mysterious story first originated, but some people believe that Dick's mother, distraught at her son's tragic death, had the remains of his car (minus the engine) brought back to his home at Pull Court and buried in the grounds, close to or under the small chapel she had built. Legend has it that she obtained the wrecked car with the assistance of Count von Ribbentrop, Hitler's Foreign Minister, who had visited Pull Court several times as a guest of the family prior to Dick's death. I have investigated this story at great length over the years and spoken with various motoring historians and the vast majority regard it as nothing more than a good bit of motorsport folklore, a complete myth. There is no hard evidence to say that the burial of the car ever took place, but to my knowledge no-one to date has carried out any scientific tests at the site using modern thermal imaging equipment, so the story for now is in limbo.

In October 1996 the newspaper *The Independent* in the UK carried a story about the mystery under the heading, 'Car fans search for the lost Mercedes of 1930s

Grand Prix ace'. It appears that Morgan Motor Company employee Maurice Owen, who lived near Pull Court in the 1930s and had met Dick Seaman, wanted to carry out tests at the manor house using modern technology; he had the backing of an American who was also interested in the story. Since that time, I don't believe any further stories have appeared in the press relating to the Dick Seaman car and the burial mystery. For the record, the manor house is now a private school.

Tony Marsh 1931–2009
Born Stourbridge (Worcestershire boundary change)
Tony Marsh is included here in this chapter relating to the county's Grand Prix connections despite the fact that he only competed in four races during his career. Tony made his grand prix debut in 1957 at the German Grand Prix, finishing fifteenth in a Cooper T43. He returned to Germany for the 1958 race, finishing eighth in a Cooper T45. In 1961 he competed in the British and German Grand Prix, driving a Lotus 18. Tony did much better when he entered the Le Man 24 Hour race in 1960, driving a Lotus Elite with John Wagstaff; the pair finished fourteenth in a very strong field, beating many famous drivers in the process.

Although Tony's Grand Prix record might not be impressive, his exploits in British hillclimb racing certainly are, as this was his speciality. Tony began his hillclimb racing with the ex-Cooper-JAP of Kidderminster's Peter Collins, winning three titles in the years 1955–57. In total Tony won six British Hillclimb Championships during his career, giving him legendary status within that arm of motorsport.

Derek Bell MBE
Educated at the King's School, Worcester
Derek Bell took part in several Grand Prix, but is best remembered for being one of the greatest endurance race drivers of all time, winning the prestigious Le Man 24 Hour race on five occasions. Derek was educated at the prestigious King's School, situated next to the cathedral in Worcester.

James Calado
Born Cropthorne, Worcestershire, 1989
James is a respected driver in the World Endurance Championship, and makes it into this Grand Prix chapter due to the fact that he was a test driver for the Force India team in the 2013 season.

Peter Douglas Conyers Walker

Born Leeds, 1912

Died Newtown, Worcester, 1984

Peter took part in several Grand Prix during his racing career, with his most notable finish being seventh place at the British Grand Prix in 1951. He drove for ERA, BRM and Maserati-Connaught between 1950 and 1955. His greatest racing achievement was winning the Le Man 24 Hour race in 1951 alongside Peter Whitehead in a C-Type Jaguar. Peter retired from racing after a crash at the 1956 Le Man race.

Rob Austin

Born Evesham, Worcestershire, 1981

Racing driver, appeared in the 2013 Ron Howard film *Rush*, about James Hunt. Rob drove a Surtees TS19 car in the film (a car owned by his father).

Colonel Sir Henry Lofft Capel-Holden, 1856–1937

Retired to Malvern, Worcestershire

Not exactly a name which rolls off the tongue in relation to Grand Prix racing, but Sir Henry will always be remembered as the designer of the iconic banked race track, Brooklands.

The Austin 7

Designed at Lickey Grange, Worcestershire

Made its motorsport debut in 1922 at the Shelsley Walsh hillclimb track, Worcestershire. Winner of the Australian Grand Prix, 1928, 1929 and 1938. Also winner of the 100 mile Australian Grand Prix of 1927, and the 1923 'Grand Prix des cycle-cars' held on the Monza circuit, Italy.

Cosworth Castings, Worcester

Cosworth is a name synonymous with motorsport. Engine blocks and heads were cast in the city and fitted to many Grand Prix winning cars.

Ward's of Worcester

Tooling company, now ceased trading

This tooling/engineering business, once located in the Blackpole area of Worcester, was an early sponsor of Frank Williams' Grand Prix team. The Ward name was carried on the ill-fated De Tomaso car of Piers Courage, in which he was tragically killed at Zandvoort, the Netherlands, in 1970.

Martin Stretton Racing
Based at Rock, near Stourport, Worcestershire
Martin Stretton is a highly respected driver who specialised in historic Grand Prix racing, winning several titles in 2002, 2004 and 2006. He is also a three-time winner of the historic Monaco Grand Prix; two of his best known ex-Grand Prix machines are the Tyrell 005 and the six-wheeled Tyrell P34.

6

Auto-Sleepers – Motorhomes of Distinction

There have been two major passions in my life outside of my family: the first is historic motor racing and the second is motorhomes, having been indoctrinated into the leisure activity by my parents in the 1960s. With my father at the wheel of a BMC converted ambulance/camper, the family enjoyed a touring holiday in France, Belgium and Holland during the late 1960s. In addition to this enjoyable foreign sojourn, my father's everyday transport happened to be a 1964 Commer Maidstone camper van, so it is hardly surprising that motorhomes were to play a huge part in my life thereafter.

This form of outdoor leisure first became popular in Europe with the introduction by Volkswagen of their Westfalia 'camping box', a rudimentary camper van based around their (then new) VW Transporter. However, it was not until the mid-1950s that this form of camping began to gain momentum in the UK. Peter Pitt, Martin Walter Ltd (Dormobile), Maurice Calthorpe and Jack White (Devon Conversions) were the first converters in Britain to produce and publicise their camping vehicles. As with any new product, when it is first introduced there is usually one firm in particular which comes to the fore, and in the case of camper vans, it was the huge Martin Walter Ltd company in Folkestone, which steadily began to take the lion's share of the new market. Their conversion based on the popular light commercial Bedford CA van became the best selling camper in the UK by the late 1950s, and the model name would become synonymous with camping vehicles in Britain, the 'Dormobile'.

As Britain recovered from the war and the economy picked up, the activity of motor caravanning blossomed to such an extent that the Martin Walter factory was having Bedford vans delivered by the train load from the Luton works where they were built. By the time the Swinging Sixties had arrived, that small list of early camper van converters had grown considerably, and the larger coachbuilt motorhomes were also selling in large numbers. It was not just the factory built camper vans which were appearing on the campsites and seaside resorts around the UK, as not everyone was able to afford, or wanted, a factory converted camper van; a great number of enthusiasts converted their own vehicles by purchasing an ex-delivery van and fitting it out with homemade furniture. One such person was a Mr Leslie Trevelyan, who lived on the Worcestershire/Gloucestershire border and constructed his own camper van (on a Morris J2 van) in order to take his wife and two sons on a holiday to France. Both the home-converted camper van and the holiday were a complete success, and on his return, Mr Trevelyan decided to make a Mk II version, this time using an Austin 152 van. The story goes that a garage owner saw this vehicle and was so impressed by it that he placed an order for five examples with Mr Trevelyan; the garage was Henlys of Bristol.

Unable to convert five vans in a short space of time, Mr Trevelyan enlisted the help of an acquaintance, Bob Halling, to work as a sub-contractor on the vehicles. The order was duly completed and further orders for more camper vans placed; the result was that a new business was formed and premises were required. A site was chosen on which to build a small factory, near the village of Willersey in Worcestershire, close to the picturesque town of Broadway. Building work was held up for a while due to the fact that the landowner, a local farmer, wanted to harvest his crop of onions off the field, but it was worth the wait, as the iconic Auto-Sleeper brand was about to be born.

The new company concentrated their efforts on producing a high quality camper van with a wooden, hand-built interior, and their own rising roof design to allow standing room within the vehicle. Within a short period of time, they began to gain a reputation for build quality, and switched from converting the BMC J2 vans to the Rootes Group Commer van. Demand was so steady for this Auto-Sleeper Commer camper van that no advertising was necessary, and the company did not convert any other make of van throughout the 1960s. The Bedford CF van was introduced in 1969, and shortly after Auto-Sleepers added this model to their catalogue, sticking with the same interior design which had proved so successful on the Commer van, together with a rising roof. These two models continued to sell well into the 1970s and cemented

Auto-Sleeper's reputation for exceptional quality and attention to detail. When the new Leyland Sherpa was unveiled in 1975, it was given the same interior as the Commer and Bedford CF, and with the Mk I Ford Transit being added to the options, it meant that customers now had four rising roof Auto-Sleepers to choose from. The company had expanded its factory facilities at Willersey, increased the workforce and was by this time producing full-colour advertising brochures for all their models.

In terms of UK motorhome converters at this time, the huge Ci/Autohomes company based in Poole and Dormobile in Folkestone were selling very large numbers of motorhomes, and both had a strong model line-up that included the larger coach-built examples. Auto-Sleepers did not introduce their first larger coach-built model until 1977, some sixteen years after the company was conceived. This model was given the name CB22 and had a single entrance rear door, toilet/shower room, a hand-built wooden interior and two double beds. Based on the Bedford CF, it was advertised as not requiring any optional extras, due to the number of features included in the standard price; for 1977 it was indeed a very luxurious motorhome, and I'm pleased to say I am the owner of one of the surviving examples from that period, which I still use regularly. The Bedford CB22 was probably the turning point for Auto-Sleepers, and launched them on their way to becoming a major player in the UK motorhome market. If some people within the industry thought that Auto-Sleeper models had been slightly conservative in their design up to that point, then they were left in amazement at the model which the company produced in 1980.

The new model was the SV100, and again was based on the Bedford CF chassis, but this time its designer, William Towns (of Aston Martin Lagonda fame), had really pushed the parameters of motorhome design, producing an all-glass fibre monocoque when the rest of the industry were still using the tried and tested build method of aluminium sheets clad over a wooden frame; the SV100 laid the foundations for the company's success through the 1980s and beyond in the coachbuilt motorhome class. With the Dormobile company in Folkestone now concentrating on welfare vehicle conversions, it was Ci/Autohomes and Auto-Sleepers who were recognised as the leading converters of motorhomes within the UK as the 1980s began. Having produced the innovative Bedford SV100 in 1980, the Worcestershire concern went from strength to strength and began to utilise several different chassis, including the Volkswagen T25 Transporter, the Renault Trafic and the Talbot Express. The 1980s would also see a plethora of new high top camper vans introduced when a glass fibre high roof fitted to a van conversion allowed occupants full standing height within the vehicle, without the need to raise a rising roof. Models introduced by Auto-Sleepers which utilised this new high roof concept included the Bedford CF CX200 and the Talbot Express CX1000; more would follow, such as the Renault Rapport, Ford Flair, Talbot Rambler and Harmony and the Talbot Rhapsody. These high top camper vans were, by the mid-1980s, accounting for a huge slice of the UK motorhome market and Auto-Sleepers, with their strong model line-up, were achieving considerable sales success. The old Leyland Sherpa had been dropped and replaced with a restyled version (the Freight Rover), onto which Auto-Sleepers added their own touch to create the Sherpa Leisure Executive. New models were appearing thick and fast from the Willersey factory and the company once considered a little conservative for their approach were now taking the UK motorhome market by storm. Winning awards left right and centre, and catering for every taste in the market from rising roof camper vans, high tops and coachbuilts.

Almost as quickly as a new light commercial van was unveiled, Auto-Sleepers would be there with a motorhome conversion; the Vauxhall Midi was announced as a camper van in high top form, as too was the larger Volkswagen, the LT; they even dipped their toes into the American van range with a conversion based on the Chevrolet van. Auto-Sleeper models were winning the 'Motorhome of the Year' award with great regularity, and were also winning gold medals from the IBCAM (Institute of British Carriage and Automobile Manufacturers). As the 1990s dawned, Auto-Sleeper were firmly entrenched as one of the leading builders of UK motorhomes, with models of every size and shape, in panel van and coach-built format, on a wide variety of chassis; they were also highly respected converters of high quality products. In October 1992 a disaster struck in the company when a fire broke out at the factory; raging throughout the night, the fire destroyed the original factory building where so many Commer vans had been converted, plus building supplies and many early factory records. Such devastation could quite easily have seen the end of the company, but such was the spirit of Managing Director Anthony Trevelyan and his dedicated staff that they had managed to start limited production in an undamaged building within a week, and one year on from the fire, full production was once again taking place at Willersey.

Anthony Trevelyan, son of Leslie the founder, had guided Auto-Sleepers through the recession of the 1980s and the fire of the 1990s, and after its main UK rival, Autohomes of Poole, closed its factory doors in the late 1990s (the Autohomes name was sold), leaving Auto-Sleepers as one of the leading motorhome converters in the country; but times were changing and many UK trailer caravan builders were by now entering the motorhome market. Anthony had opened up export markets to France, Luxemburg, Germany, Switzerland, New Zealand, Australia and Japan; Auto-Sleepers were a world-wide brand. Anthony's brother Charles was to oversee the opening of a service centre at Willersey, where buyers of their products could get a vehicle service, have repairs carried out, and have a host of optional extras fitted by trained staff.

By 2000 Auto-Sleepers had merged with the motorhome dealer Marquis, and by 2005 had made a further merger with the SeA Group of European motorhome producers, in effect taking what was a family company out of British ownership. Managing Director Anthony Trevelyan eventually retired, leaving his brother Charles as the sole surviving Trevelyan family member, who was running the service centre at the factory. Anthony later re-appeared in the motorhome industry to work for the Swift Group as Director of External Affairs; Charles retired from Auto-Sleepers in 2009.

In 2009 Auto-Sleepers returned to British ownership when Geoff Scott and Mike Crouch became equal partners in the company. Trailer caravans have since been added to the products produced at the Willersey factory, though at the present time, that long list of available Auto-Sleeper models of motorhomes has been reduced drastically from that seen during the 1980s.

Auto-Sleepers have the distinction of being the only motorhome manufacturer to have one of their products on permanent display at the National Motor Museum at Beaulieu. The 1964 Commer is a wonderful example of the company's hand-crafted early camper vans; showing just 22,000 miles from new, it was donated to the museum by its original owner.

Left: The high-tech pit area at Silverstone as it is today. (Photo courtesy James Prosser)

Below: A familiar sight to many regular visitors to the old Silverstone circuit, the *Daily Express* Bridge.

Richard 'Dick' Seaman, Grand Prix racing driver with the Mercedes team during the 1950s. Tales exist of how his mother had his crashed Mercedes brought back to his home at Pull Court, and buried it in the grounds. However, records do show that the car was dismantled back at the factory, and some parts reused. So unless just some pieces of the bodywork were buried, the whole tale is highly unlikely.

The very grand Pull Court, pictured around the late 1920s, the home of racing driver Dick Seaman.

Madresfield Court near Malvern has hosted speed trials on its estate for many years, the long Gloucester Drive through the grounds has been host to several Grand Prix cars and drivers down the years.

Auto-Sleepers of Willersey, near Broadway, have been producing some of Britain's finest motorhomes at their Orchard Works since 1961.

MOTORIZED CARAVAN ADDITION

NEW 3/4-BERTH CONVERSION FOR AUSTIN 152, MORRIS J2 OR COMMER

Above: When the elevating roof is lowered its side panels fold inwards, and the roof "parallelograms" forward with its hinged end pieces. Left: There is an additional shallow locker attached to the rear door; bedding may be stowed beneath the bench seats

OVER the past year a limited number of caravan conversions have been carried out to special order by a Cheltenham firm—Auto-Sleepers Ltd.—and the basic design has been improved progressively. Now, production is being increased, and the conversion is added to the list of makes available, bringing to 22 the new total of manufacturers engaged in this work.

Recently a visit was made to Cheltenham to examine this new motorized caravan, and it was found to offer several particularly good features, and to set an extremely high standard of quality in its construction. The Morris J2 16/18 cwt was inspected, but the conversion is also available on the Austin 152, and in slightly modified form on the Commer 15 cwt.

In the driving compartment two seats with flat squabs and cushions convert to form a single child's bed across the width of the vehicle. This compartment can then be cut off by curtains from the main part of the caravan, in which two facing bench seats set to the right of the van fold flat to form a double bed. At extra cost of £18 10s a full-length folding bunk is provided

to attach securely some four feet above the double bed, and with this accessory the Auto-Sleeper will accommodate three adults and one child.

Space for use of the upper bunk is provided by an elevating roof which is part of the standard equipment, and comprises a large Fibreglass panel with hinged end pieces, which in side view tilts to its raised position with a parallelogram" action. The side panels are then swung into place, and may be secured slightly open on one side, allowing generous ventilation.

A cooker with two rings and a grill is built in above a large locker well forward on the left, and the sink in unit with the draining board is on the same side at the rear of the van. Water delivery is by combined pump and tap from a galvanized iron tank with exterior filler. Water storage capacity is 16 gallons, making this the first motorized caravan on the British market to allow really adequate fresh water tankage for four.

The table mounts securely from the right wall, and as a second function bridges the gap between the two facing bench seats when the double bed is made up. All seats are upholstered in thick foam rubber and are faced with cloth on one side and hard-wearing p.v.c. on the reverse. A wardrobe is on the right of the van at the back.

Lino covers the entire floor area, and all the woodwork is of oak-faced ply or solid oak. Cupboard doors are secured when closed by double catches, and the set of drawers near the side door are finished to a fine interference fit, to remain firmly closed by their own friction—an indication of the high quality of workmanship in construction of this caravan. Lighting is by three electric lamps, supplementing the standard electric light over the driving cab. There is a fixed rear step.

Distributors are Wicliffe Motor Company of Cheltenham, Henlys of Bristol, and Halesowen Motor Works of Halesowen. The prices are £889 (B.M.C.), £895 (Commer). An additional model on the B.M.C. J4 van is planned. The address of Auto-Sleepers Ltd. is Wood Stanway, Cheltenham, Gloucestershire.

Child's bed setup in the front compartment, shown with the curtains half drawn. The van inspected was fitted with the new floor gear change now fitted to all B.M.C. 1½-litre vans

Generously large double bed, with the optional single bunk in position above. A mirror is provided above the drawers seen on the right, and beyond it is the sink

An early magazine review of their first model, a rising roof camper based on the Austin 152 van.

This is the very first home-converted camper built by Mr Trevelyan Sr.

The company stopped using the Austin base chassis by 1963 and concentrated purely on the Rootes Commer 1500FC vehicle. The ingenious, solid-sided lift up roof was a very distinctive feature of their conversions, and is still offered on one of their models today.

Auto-Sleepers built their fine reputation on the quality and craftsmanship of their early examples, and that tradition continues in the modern workshops to this day.

he company continued to convert only the Commer van throughout the 1960s, and added the Bedford CF to
eir range as the 1970s arrived.

Close-up of the distinctive Auto-Sleeper roof, with its wooden sides, eye-level windows and a glass fibre roc capping. The roof has been fitted to their Commer, Bedford CF, Ford Transit, Renault and VW conversions ove the years.

This is the Renault Auto-Sleeper Rimini, based on the MKI Renault Trafic van.

Classic Auto-Sleeper models have a terrific following; this Bedford CF was treated to a complete rebuild by its caring owner, and given a custom paint job.

The Worcestershire company have carried out motorhome conversions on just about every marque of light commercial over the years; seen here is their high top Vauxhall Midi camper.

Opposite top: Auto-Sleeper unveiled their first coachbuilt model in 1977; the Bedford CB22, based on the Bedford CF chassis. Seen here is the author's classic motorhome dating from 1978, and still giving excellent service.

Opposite bottom: Interior of the Bedford CB22 model showing the quality of the wooden interior furniture produced by craftsmen at the Orchard Works, Willersey.

Left: The Auto-Sleeper Clubman was quite a radical departure from the traditional motorhome construction techniques; with an all glass fibre monocoque body, eliminating the need for joints.

Below: The older Auto-Sleeper models are a firm favourite today with classic motorhome fans; Bedford Clubman and Talbot Talisman motorhomes are seen here at a classic motorhome rally.

nother classic rally scene featuring a variety of older Auto-Sleeper examples, including Renault Rimini, Talbot ambler and Sportsman.

Quality control has always played an important part of the Auto-Sleeper conversion process; seen here are row of the Talbot Talisman models being checked carefully prior to despatch to customers.

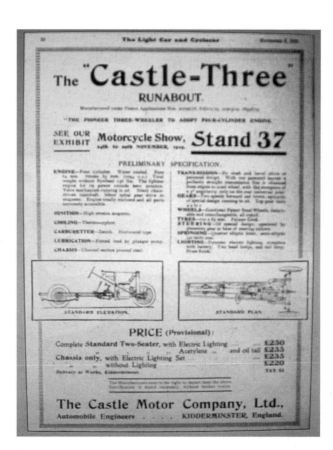

ght: An early advertisement for the
stle-Three in the Light Car and Cyclecar
agazine.

low: 'Distinction and Satisfaction' are the
rds the company used to sell their Castle-
ree in this period advert; price given was
25 complete.

This must now rank as one of the rarest exhibits at the Hartlebury Museum in Worcestershire; a survivi
example of the Kidderminster-built Castle-Three car.

The late George Spears seen here competing at a winter trial in 1950 in his MKI prototype Dellow.

The Dellow is, and always was, an ideal trials car; seen in competition here is Richard Andrews in his 1949 MKI prototype.

Mike Pearson competing in a trial at Shelsley Walsh in his Dellow; proof that Shelsley is not just about speeding up the hill against the clock, the hills have other uses.

ellow owners and their beloved cars enjoying their annual gathering at Shelsley Walsh.

The Dellow Register members are an extremely devoted and enthusiastic group of classic car owners, alway willing to chat about these rare models; this is their display stand at the Race Retro show in 2013.

he 1952 MK2A Dellow owned by Dellow Register Honorary Secretary Mr Bob Broughton.

Top: The personal Dellow of Lionel Evans.

Above: LAB 274, often referred to as the Morgan-Dellow, when in fact a more correct title would be a Morga[n]
Radpanels, as the bodywork was the creation of Lionel Evans at Radpanels, who did just happen to make t[he]
bodywork for the Dellow cars.

The custom-built +4 Morgan is taken up the hill at Shelsley Walsh in the early 1950s; it would change ownership several times over the years before ending up with a dealership who sold it to a Morgan collector in the USA. He owned it very briefly before selling it at auction.

Resplendent in new green paintwork after a near full restoration prior to being shipped to the USA; it wa displayed at the Concours d'Elegance in Santa Barbara before being sold at the Scottsdale Auction for aroun $79,000 a couple of years ago.

Right: An early print of the McNaught factory in Worcester.

Below: Carmichael of Worcester have built a reputation over several decades as one of the best manufacturers of fire tenders in the UK; early examples pictured here outside Malvern Fire Station in Howsell Road (building remains but station has moved).

Top: More Carmichael appliances, this time outside Leicester Central *c.* 1990.

Above: Matt Neal at the wheel of his Honda touring car; a familiar sight to the thousands of BTC enthusias[?] who attend races all over the UK.

Opposite page: The hugely talented figure of Matt Neal; one of the most popular drivers in the British Tourir[?] Car Championship.

It's a place of work, but not as most people know it; Rob Austin is certainly well protected in his race car.

On the podium is where Rob's many fans enjoy seeing him on race days.

Rob doing a wheelie in his BTCC Audi.

The author enjoys his first taste of motoring, 1950s agricultural style.

7

Motor Manufacturers in the County

I believe that it was only fitting and proper to commence this book by featuring two of the most prominent Worcestershire car manufacturers, Morgan and Santler. My reasoning was that Morgan is a car brand still recognised around the world today, whereas Santler, by no means a household name even in the UK, is credited with building the first car in Britain. The Austin Motor Company has been given its rightful place within this title, as the Longbridge factory was actually located within the county of Worcestershire when it first began trading. But these three names are not the only car manufacturers to have an association with the county; there were more.

Castle-Three Motor Company

The name of this small company originated from the fact that its premises were located at Castle Mill Works, New Road, Kidderminster, close to Caldwell Castle; a castle was also incorporated into the radiator grille badge on its vehicles. Very little is known about this company, only that which can be found in old gazetteers, directories and county records, which show that the business originally opened as a repair garage around 1906, and entered into the manufacture of munitions for the First World War from 1914–18. By 1919 the company were embarking upon the construction of a three-wheeled cyclecar, not dissimilar to those produced by Morgan and Santler a few miles south in Malvern.

The first examples produced were fitted with four-cylinder water-cooled engines, originally of 1,094 cc, although some later models were upgraded to a

1,207 cc unit. Both two and three speed gearboxes were fitted, driving the single rear wheel by means of a shaft. Bodywork was of the open, two-seater form with dickey seat, with the car's somewhat strange appearance due to the fitting of artillery-style wheels as opposed to wire spoke wheels, which were normal at that time. The cyclecar was exhibited at the motor show of 1919, but despite quite a lot of interest, and reportedly many orders being taken, it is believed that fewer than 400 were ever built. Only two examples are known to survive, one of which is on display at the County Museum at Hartlebury, mid-distance between Worcester and Kidderminster.

The company did design and build a prototype four-wheeled car, but it failed to make it into production; the company ceased trading around 1922. The name of the company was given a new lease of life recently when the Castle Three Motor Company Limited was incorporated in Alnwick, Northumberland; they announced plans to build a modern version of the three-wheeled cyclecar.

Dellow

The name of this company was imaginatively conceived by joining together the surnames of its founders, Ken Delingpole and Ron Lowe; the company operated between the late 1940s and 1950s from premises at Alvechurch, to the north of the county. Originally started as a specialist car tuning enterprise, Dellow Motors was also an agent for Ventnor superchargers and the HRG sports cars. The sport of 'trials' was a very popular arm of motorsport throughout the first half of the twentieth century, and Ron Lowe was a keen participant. One of his early trial cars was based around an Austin 7, and during the 1947 season he made modifications to it which included the fitting of a Ford side-valve engine; he even added Ford axles at a later date. Ron's highly modified car became known in trials as the 'Flipper', and the car did bring Ron plenty of success in the sport. The car became the basis for Dellow cars, which were built using the Austin 7 chassis and the running gear from Ford vehicles. To this the garage welded a tubular steel frame, and clad it in aluminium to produce a body, this task being entrusted to Kidderminster-based Radpanels, run by Lionel Evans.

The trials success of these early Dellow machines would lead the company to start producing cars with new Ford parts rather than recycled ones, and they began to build their own chassis using high quality tubular chromium molybdenum. Dellow cars were an instant success and within the first year of production around sixty had been built, leading to the introduction of the Mk II by the following year. The year 1951 would be a significant one in Dellow history as Walter Waring won the RAC Trials Championship with a WHW-Dellow Special. That year production of Dellow cars had increased to over seventy examples and by 1952 a Mk III was introduced, longer than the previous model and this time a four-seater. At this point in the Dellow tale it is worth recalling that two Worcestershire drivers already mentioned in the Grand Prix chapter, namely Peter Collins and Tony Marsh, were early drivers of Dellow cars in trials and hillclimb competitions.

By 1952 sales figures were dropping for Dellow cars, a trend repeated the following year, though in competitions Dellow were doing extremely well, winning the Daily Express Rally in 1952 and twice winning the Circuit of Ireland Trial. By 1954 the Mk IV Dellow appeared, now fitted with the recently released Ford 100E engine; this was in effect a production version of the special hillclimb car built for, and used by, Tony Marsh. Falling sales (only fifteen examples were sold in 1955) did eventually lead to Dellow being sold in 1956 to a trials competitor and enthusiast, Neville Nightingale; this in turn would see Dellow renamed as Dellow Engineering Limited, and the factory moved from Alvechurch, Worcestershire, to Oldbury. The manufacturing of Dellow cars at the new site was not a huge success, and although the cars did continue to be sold up to 1959, the new company was enjoying a great degree of business from general repairs, specialist services and continuing to provide owners of Dellow cars with spares. It is widely accepted that the complete production figure for all Dellow cars did not exceed 300.

That small factory just off Latimer Road, Alvechurch, may no longer exist but due to the fact that the chassis of later models were made from ex-government rocket casings and the bodies were constructed using aluminium, a large number of Dellow examples have survived to the present day, in excess of 200 it is believed. One such example has a very interesting history: chassis number P2440, with the registration number LAB 274.

In the aftermath of the Second World War, metal was in short supply and many car manufacturers had to comply with government guidelines with regard to exports. An Ombersley man by the name of Graeme Anton visited the Morgan Motor Company in Malvern with a view to ordering a +4 Morgan car, but was informed by Peter Morgan that although the basic chassis with running gear was not a problem, the bodywork on the other hand was. Graeme approached Radpanels of Oxford Street, Kidderminster, to see if they could fit his rolling Morgan chassis with bodywork; they informed him that this was possible as they had done a similar Morgan for a Pershore customer already. Mr Anton had been injured during the war and required modifications to whatever doors were fitted to enable him to get in and out of the car a little more easily. Radpanels fitted the metal bodywork over a tubular frame, as opposed to the ash frame Morgan would have used, and the doors were hinged at the rear. As Radpanels were the company who fitted bodywork to the Dellow cars, Mr Anton's car did resemble a cross between a Dellow and a Morgan; it was delivered to Mr Anton in September 1952.

The Dellow-Morgan (as it has become known) was used by Mr Anton on a regular basis for both road use and in sporting trials and hillclimbs, including the famous Shelsely Walsh. When the car was eventually sold, it passed to a Morgan enthusiast, Quentin English (of the Morgan Club), who also used the car for a variety of sporting events, including trials and sprints. It then passed through the hands of a couple more owners, and spent some years sitting unused. LAB 274 resurfaced once more in 1991 when it was acquired by Morgan agent Melvyn Rutter, though by this time it was in a poor state mechanically and required the cylinder block to be replaced. Fast forward a couple more owners, and into the mid-2000s the Dellow-Morgan ended up in the ownership of Dennis Glavis, a Morgan collector in the USA. He sold the car at the Scottsdale Auction in 2012 for the sum of $79,750.

Enfield Autocar Company

The name Enfield is one of those magical trade names from the era of the British Empire, a name associated with guns, cycles and, most famously, British motorcycles. Not a brand name one would immediately associate with the motor car, and yet the Redditch-based company had toyed with some forms of quadricycles, and one of their early examples is thought to have been Henry Royce's first vehicle. By 1904 the company had begun to build motor cars, beginning with two models, one being a 6-hp two-seater example with a De Dion engine, and the other a 10-hp vehicle, a four-seater with a twin cylinder engine. In 1906 car building was separated from the cycle and motorcycle manufacture when the Enfield Autocar Company was formed, and immediately larger, more complex vehicles were being designed by E. H. Lancaster.

Within just two years of separating from parent company Royal Enfield, the Enfield Autocar Company was sold to Alldays & Onions Pneumatic Engineering Company Ltd of Sparkbrook, Birmingham, and production was re-located from the Worcestershire factory; cars manufactured after this time were given the name 'Enfield-Alldays'.

V. P. Webb & Company Ltd

This was a very small car manufacturer based in Stourport on Severn, Worcestershire, and traded for only around two years, *c.* 1922/3. Founded by Victor Webb, the company produced the 'Sensational Super-Nine', which was a 8.9-hp, four-cylinder car fitted with a 1.1-litre engine; less than 100 examples are believed to have been built.

McNaught & Company

Mr J. A. McNaught, born in Kendal in 1828, was the son of a coachbuilder. He entered into the profession himself, working for several firms before arriving in the city of Worcester in 1956 and going into partnership with a Mr Kinder, himself a coachbuilder from the Tything area. Mr Kinder eventually retired from the business and was succeeded firstly by a Mr Lamb-Smith, and then a Mr J. Aldren. Having begun the coachbuilding business constructing horse-drawn traps and carriages, they quickly gained a reputation for producing items of exceptional quality, and expanded into the building of much larger coaches. The business expanded rapidly, as did the workforce, and they began to win gold medals at major exhibitions such as London, Paris and Sydney. McNaught & Company were by this time building a world-wide reputation and were commissioned to build the Lord Mayor's coach for London, county Sheriffs' coaches and one for HRH the Prince of Wales. I'm proud to say that in among those prestigious clients was my great-grandfather, who owned Mildenham Mill; he had a carriage built by McNaughts as the family transport.

With the advent of the motor car in the early twentieth century, the company turned their attention to building bodywork onto car chassis, as early cars had wooden framework. In their catalogue dated 1904, they featured illustrated designs for a 'Side-Light Motor Brougham', a Single Landaulette, a side-entrance Phaeton, a Roi-des-Belges and a Motor Omnibus. They later constructed taxi bodies onto various chassis, and had by then opened showrooms in London,

Liverpool and Birmingham. One of their famous local customers was C. W. Dyson Perrins of Malvern, who owned a whole stable of cars. He wrote to McNaught & Co. from his large house, Davenham, in Malvern in 1911, saying:

> I am pleased to be able to say that the work which you have done for me for many years past has always given me the fullest satisfaction, which is mainly due to the personal care you take in whatever is entrusted to you. I can give no better testimonial (except by continuing to give you my work, which I certainly hope to do) than by saying that I have today written to the Secretary of the Royal Automobile Club in answer to an official enquiry, and that I consider you are worthy of the highest certificate which they issue.

By the mid-1930s the company had ceased trading, no doubt partly as a consequence of all-metal bodywork on motor cars, though other long-established coachbuilders around the UK found other avenues to explore for their workforce and skills.

Amdac Carmichael

The Carmichael company began as a specialist coachbuilding concern in 1849, concentrating mainly on hand-crafted carriages at that time; the company expanded into creating bodywork for agricultural appliances in the early twentieth century. Called upon by the government to produce fire pumps for use during the Second World War, this was to become a niche sales market for the company from 1947. They produced their first fire tender for Worcester fire brigade, and by 1952 had exported their first tender to New Zealand. Carmichael expanded its range of fire fighting vehicles, and by 1962 had sold its first specialised airfield tender, a market in which they remain strong today, with Carmichael appliances in use at airports all over the world.

The company have been successfully building, supplying and exporting their fire fighting vehicles for several decades, and remain one of the leading UK concerns in this field.

Miscellanea of People, Places and Facts

Other Motorsport Links with the County

The county has strong links with motorsport, notably Grand Prix racing and hillclimbing, as already mentioned; though other branches of the sport are well represented. Rallying has a huge following, not only in the UK but throughout the world, and Worcestershire can proudly boast that it has one of the very best from the 1970s and 80s as a long-time resident. Russell Brookes, born in Redditch in 1945, finished on the podium three times in the RAC Rally in 1977–79, and was crowned British Rally Champion in 1977 driving a Ford Escort RS1800. He will be remembered by UK rally fans during the 1980s for driving the fabulous Ford Sierra RS Cosworth and the 4x4 Ford Sapphire Cosworth. Russell retired from rally driving in the early 90s, but still takes part in historic races and rallys occasionally.

Another branch of motorsport with strong county connections is the British Touring Car Championship (BTCC), and teams don't get much bigger or better than Team Dynamics, who are based in Pershore. Formed in 1991, the Worcestershire-based team have an incredible fan base throughout the UK, and to date have won twenty titles. Famous drivers for the team include the 2012 BTCC Champion, Gordon Sneddon, and Matt Neal, champion in 2005, 2006 and 2011.

Evesham can lay claim to being the birthplace of BTCC driver Rob Austin, who was born in the town in February 1981. Rob has raced in a variety of championships over the years, which include Formula Renault, British F3,

British GT, Seat Cupra, F3 Euro Series, Ginetta G50, the Grand Prix Masters
in 2010, and the VW Cup in 2012. Rob's father is a well known participant in
historic racing, as he owns a former Team Surtees TS19 Grand Prix car, which
Rob drove during the filming of *Rush*, the Ron Howard film about the career
of James Hunt. Rob Austin finished eleventh in the BTCC in 2013.

Capt. George Thomas Smith-Clarke

Born Bewdley, Worcestershire, 1884

Died Coventry 1960

George Smith-Clarke was born at 6 Lower Park, Bewdley, Worcestershire,
served an apprenticeship on the railways and joined the Royal Flying Corps
in 1916, progressing to the rank of captain by 1917. After the war he became
the Works Manager at Daimler, and in 1922 was appointed Works Manager
of Alvis cars. Along with W. M. Dunn, he was responsible for the design of the
Alvis Speed 20 and 25 sports cars, together with several notable engines. He
also played a major part in the design of breathing apparatus for the medical
profession. He retired from Alvis in 1950, and passed away at his home in
Coventry in 1960. The local Civic Society has now placed a blue plaque on the
birthplace of Smith-Clarke in Bewdley.

Geoffrey Dummer MBE

1909–2002

Geoffrey Dummer was an electronics engineer who moved to Malvern in the 1930s
in order to take up a position with the Air Ministry at the Research Establishment
(later to become TRE, RRE and RSRE). A great deal of top secret electronic and
radar work was carried out on sites in and around Malvern during the Second
World War and beyond. Geoffrey Dummer will be forever remembered as the
genius who was the first to conceptualise (and build a prototype of) an integrated
circuit board, better known today as the microchip. Although Geoffrey Dummer
was not directly linked with motoring history, he is included because the modern
microchip is used to build new cars throughout the world today.

Heenan & Froude

Worcester engineering company

Heenan & Froude was originally a Manchester-based engineering business,
which also had a factory in Birmingham. The company eventually moved

its HQ to a large factory site at Shrub Hill, Worcester, covering a vast area close to the railway station. The company were responsible for the building of the Blackpool Tower, and the factories at Longbridge for the Austin Motor Company. They specialised in the manufacture of water dynamometers for testing purposes, together with valves and sundry items for the rail industry. In the early part of the twentieth century, STD Motors acquired residual shares in Heenean & Froude, which meant that a motoring manufacturer in the form of Sunbeam-Talbot-Darracq (STD Motors) then had extremely strong links to the city of Worcester, despite the fact that none of those cars were built in the city.

By 1935 STD Motors had gone bankrupt, and by 1937 the former, once large Heenans factory had become five splinter factories, owned by seven different companies, though the main Heenan & Froude company name did remain intact. They continued to specialise in dynamometers for engine testing, supplying several car manufacturers, including the giant Vauxhall Motors factory at Luton. In 1968 another Worcester engineering business merged with Heenan & Froude to form Redman Heenan Froude Ltd. By the 1980s Froude Engineering was part of the Babcock International Group, being sold to FKI Group in 1987.

Today, more than 100 years after they began building water dynamometers, the Froude-Hofmann factory at Worcester are now making extremely high-tech engine and chassis testing equipment at a new site to the north of the city centre. The original Heenean & Froude factory buildings remain, flanking the approach road to Shrub Hill railway station, but they now house a multitude of different trades.

Hydro Aluminium Worcester

Based in the Shrub Hill area of the city, this company are a subsidiary of Holden Aluminium Technologies Ltd. They build full body structures and crash management systems for such famous names as Aston-Martin, BMW, Jaguar and Lotus.

Reg Job

Morris Minor design team member

I was fortunate to interview the late Reg Job for a magazine at his home in Fernhill Heath during the early 1990s. Reg was an integral part of the design team who were responsible for the famous Morris Minor, and worked alongside

Sir Alec Issigonis for many years. Sadly, due to his wife's ill health, I didn't get to spend as much time talking to him as I would have liked, but he was a truly fascinating character, and immensely proud of his design achievements.

It simply is not possible, within the confines of a title of this size, to cover every single business, company and person who played even a minor part in the history of motoring within the county during the last 100 years and more. In covering the most famous, celebrated and well known facets of county motoring, I am aware that I am doing a disservice to many contributing businesses such as Terry's Springs, Garringtons, Wards, Britax, and Windshields of Worcester to name but very few. I have also omitted the huge motorcycle industry within the county, such as Royal Enfield and many more, but one could easily write a whole book on the subject of the county's connections with motorcycling since its inception. With such a wealth of motoring related names, places, sports people and businesses to choose from, I really have been spoilt for choice and have had to therefore be selective.

Acknowledgements

I would like to say a huge thanks to several people who have very kindly assisted me by providing photographs for this book; their help and assistance has been invaluable.

Morgan Motor Company (Martyn Webb, archivist), A. B. Demaus, Chris Price, Louise Collins-King Collection, Terry Acreman, Phil Loughton Photography, Clive S. Shearman Collection, The Dellow Register, Nick Turley, Pre-War Austin 7 Club Ltd, Team Dynamics, Jakab Ebery Photographic, Graeme Anton, Richard Clement, Gene Bussian (USA), June Firkins, Rodney Evans Collection and Conceptcarz.